FEEDING YOUR DEMONS

ALSO BY TSULTRIM ALLIONE

Women of Wisdom

FEEDING

YOUR

DEMONS

ANCIENT WISDOM FOR
RESOLVING INNER CONFLICT

TSULTRIM ALLIONE
FOREWORD BY JACK KORNFIELD

LITTLE, BROWN AND COMPANY
NEW YORK   BOSTON   LONDON

Little, Brown and Company
Hachette Book Group
1290 Avenue of the Americas, New York, NY 10104
littlebrown.com

First Edition: April 2008

Little, Brown and Company is a division of Hachette Book Group, Inc.
The Little, Brown name and logo are trademarks of Hachette Book Group, Inc.

The publisher is not responsible for websites (or their content)
that are not owned by the publisher.

This book is intended to supplement, not replace, the advice of a trained mental or physical health professional. If you know or suspect that you have a mental health problem, you should consult a health professional. If you have a physical health problem, we also recommend that you continue your treatment and follow the advice of your doctor. The author and publisher specifically disclaim any liability, loss, or risk, personal or otherwise, which is incurred as a consequence, directly or indirectly, of the use and application of any of the contents of this book.

Jérôme Edou, "Machig's Last Instructions" from Machig Labdrön and the Foundations of Chöd. Copyright © 1995. Reprinted with the permission of Snow Lion Publications, www.snowlionpub.com.

Library of Congress Cataloging-in-Publication Data

Allione, Tsultrim.
    Feeding your demons : ancient wisdom for resolving inner conflict / Tsultrim Allione.
        p.   cm.
    Includes index.
    ISBN-13: 978-0-316-01313-0
    ISBN-10: 0-316-01313-7
        1. Spiritual life — Buddhism.   I. Title.
    BQ5660.A55 2008
    294.3'444 — dc22   2007042277

10

LSC-C

Printed in the United States of America

For my precious mother, Ruth,
who has been a radiant example of compassion and
unconditional love throughout my life, and
for the Great Mother, Prajnaparamita,
the skylike mind, our true nature

CONTENTS

CONTENTS

FOREWORD

THERE ARE statues of fierce demons standing guard at the gates of most Buddhist temples. To enter the sacred space of the temple you must pass directly between them. This is because all humans, each of us, must come to terms with the demons of fear, aggression, temptation, ignorance, and their cohorts if we are to live a free and sacred life. They cannot be neglected.

In *Feeding Your Demons* Tsultrim Allione has performed a remarkable feat of cultural translation and offered the Western world a new treasure. She has taken a great and relatively unknown ancient lineage of practice and rendered it into accessible modern form without compromising its essence or losing its power. In this she brings to bear the depth of her forty years of Buddhist training, her skills as an accomplished lama and a visionary, her sophisticated understanding of the Western psyche, and her fearless consciousness, steeped in the two worlds of classical Tibet and modern life.

The need for transformation of our demons is universal. We all suffer at times from our personal demons, whether those of confusion, anger, self-hatred, trauma, longing, or loss. Collectively the force of these same demons creates enormous suffering on earth, including continuing war, racism, environmental devastation, and widespread yet unnecessary hunger and illness. To alleviate these forms of suffering, we humans will have to face the demons of greed, hatred, and delusion at their root. No amount of political or scientific change will end these sufferings unless we also learn to work with our demons, individually and collectively. Here, in the straightforward teaching offered by Tsultrim Allione, is a powerful method to do so. With exquisite detail and accuracy she shows us how we can transform the energy of addiction, shame, illness, anxiety, fear, and anger into the energy of liberation.

This transformation is at the very heart of Buddhist realization, the discovery that liberation can be found exactly where we are — not by avoiding the sufferings of life, but by turning toward them with a great heart of compassion. And by releasing our personal grasping of them, we can learn to transform their energy and find freedom in their midst.

Buddhist history tells us that after many years of teaching, the Buddha invited his most awakened followers to carry the lamp of the teachings of liberation and compassion across the world. He instructed them to translate these teachings into the vernacular of each new land so that they could bring benefit to all.

In *Feeding Your Demons* Tsultrim Allione has done so, beautifully. May the blessings and liberation offered by these practices of transforming the demons free your own heart, benefit all beings, and lead to the repair and awakening of the world. May it be so.

JACK KORNFIELD
Spirit Rock Meditation Center

FEEDING YOUR DEMONS

INTRODUCTION

FEEDING OUR DEMONS rather than fighting them might seem to contradict the conventional Western approach to what assails us, but it turns out to be a remarkably effective path to inner peace and liberation. Demons are our obsessions and fears, chronic illnesses, or common problems like depression, anxiety, and addiction. They are not bloodthirsty ghouls waiting for us in dark places; they are within us, the forces that we fight inside ourselves. They are inner enemies that undermine our best intentions. The approach of giving form to these inner forces, and feeding rather than struggling against them, was originally articulated by an eleventh-century female Buddhist teacher, Machig Labdrön (1055–1145). Her exact dates are debatable and vary according to the source, but most scholars agree she was born in 1055 and lived well into her nineties. Her spiritual practice was called Chöd (pronounced "chuh"), which means "to cut through." She developed this form of meditation, unusual even in her time in Tibet, and it generated such amazing results that it became very popular, spreading to all the schools of Tibetan Buddhism and beyond.

In today's world we suffer from record levels of inner and outer struggle, and find ourselves ever more polarized politically and spiritually. We need a new paradigm, a fresh approach to conflict. Machig's strategy of nurturing rather than battling our inner and outer enemies offers a revolutionary path to resolve conflict that leads to psychological integration and inner peace.

In 1967, at age nineteen, I had the good fortune to travel to India and Nepal and meet the Tibetans who had settled there as refugees after being forced into exile during Communist China's invasion of Tibet. I fell in love with the Tibetans and returned to India in 1969 after spending six months at the first Tibetan monastery in Scotland, founded by Chögyam Trungpa Rinpoche. In 1970 I was ordained as a Buddhist nun in the Tibetan tradition by His Holiness the Sixteenth Karmapa, in Bodhgaya, India, and for the next few years I had the immeasurable blessing of receiving teachings at the feet of many great Buddhist masters trained in Tibet. As I describe in the following pages, after several years I made the decision to return my monastic vows. It was at this time of great transition and uncertainty that I was first introduced to Chöd. I subsequently returned to America, became a mother, and sought to integrate Tibetan wisdom into my life as a layperson. I was eventually guided to discover Machig Labdrön's biography (written in Tibetan), and her teachings became pivotal for me.

Because I myself was able to find such enormous relevance in Machig's teachings, I was motivated to find a way to make her approach accessible in a Western context. When I began to teach the Chöd practice in the West, I developed an exercise of visualizing, dialoguing with, and feeding demons that yielded tangible results. Gradually from this exercise the five-step process described here evolved into a method I call feeding your demons, which began to be used independently of the Tibetan Chöd practice by my students. For the past twenty-five years—most recently at our Colorado retreat center, Tara Mandala, in Chöd and in Kapala Training retreats—I have taught this way of feeding your demons to make friends with that which we would most like to avoid.

Those who have used the method report that chronic emotional and physical issues such as anxiety, compulsive eating, panic attacks, and illness were resolved or significantly benefited from this approach. The five-step process has also proved helpful in dealing with short-term upheavals such as the breakup of a relationship, the stress of losing a job, the death of a loved one, and interpersonal problems at work and at home. Sometimes the results have been instantaneous and seemed nothing short of miraculous, while other effects have been more gradual and subtle.

The method that I call feeding your demons—based on the principles of Chöd—is a simple five-step practice that doesn't require any knowledge of Buddhism or of any Tibetan spiritual practices. In the first step we find where in the body we hold our "demon" most strongly. This demon might be addiction, self-hatred, perfectionism, anger, jealousy, or anything that is dragging you down, draining your energy. To put it simply, our demons are what we fear. As Machig said, anything that blocks complete inner freedom is a demon. She also spoke of gods and god-demons. Gods are our hopes, what we are obsessed with, what we long for, our attachments. God-demons occur when a hope and a fear are closely attached to each other; when we shift back and forth between hope and fear, this is a god-demon. Although in the following pages I refer for the most part to demons, the same approach applies equally well to our gods and god-demons.

In the second step we allow the energy that we find in the body to take personified form as a demon right in front of us. In the third step we discover what the demon needs by putting ourself in the demon's place, becoming the demon. In the fourth step we imagine dissolving our own body into nectar of whatever it is that the demon needs, and we let this flow to the demon. In this way we nurture it, feeding it to complete satisfaction. Having satisfied the demon, we find that the energy that was tied up in the demon turns into an ally. This ally offers us protection and support and then dissolves into us. At the end of the fourth step, we dissolve into emptiness, and in the fifth and final step, we simply rest in the open awareness that comes from dissolving into emptiness.

Paradoxically, feeding our gods or demons to complete satisfaction does not strengthen them; rather it allows the energy that has been locked up in them to become accessible. In this way highly charged emotions that have been bottled up by inner conflict are released and become something beneficial. When we try to fight against or repress the disowned parts of ourselves that I call demons, they actually gain power and develop resistance. In feeding our demons we are not only rendering them harmless; we are also, by addressing them instead of running away from them, nurturing the shadow parts of ourselves, so that the energy caught in the struggle transforms into a positive protective force.

Giving our demons form by personifying them brings inchoate energies or harmful habitual patterns into view, allowing them to be liberated rather than leaving them as invisible destructive forces. The alternative to feeding our demons is to engage in a conflict we can never win: our unfed demons only become more and more powerful and monstrous as we either openly battle them or remain ignorant of their undercover operations.

Although the therapeutic technique of personifying a fear or neurosis is not unfamiliar in Western psychology, the five-step practice of feeding your demons takes this approach deeper. Its additional value lies in dissolving our own bodies and nurturing rather than just personifying and interacting with our inner enemies, and in the experience of nondual meditative awareness that occurs in the final step of the process. This is a state of relaxed awareness, free from our usual fixation of "self" versus "other," which takes us beyond the place where normal psychotherapy ends.

Finding appropriate ways to bring the ancient wisdom of Tibet into the contemporary world is a challenge that anyone deeply involved in the tradition must confront. At a 1996 conference in Dharamsala, India, with His Holiness the Fourteenth Dalai Lama, I was asked to present the practice of feeding your demons in a session devoted to new methods for teaching Buddhism in the West. I had the great honor of leading the Dalai Lama, a group of distinguished lamas (Tibetan Buddhist teachers) from various traditions, and my Western colleagues through a version of the five-step practice you will learn in this book. Afterward His Holiness was very encouraging, and several Western teachers adopted this method and used it in their own retreats.

This experience reinforced my sense that all Buddhist teachers, both Eastern and Western, grapple with questions about how to most effectively present the Buddha's teachings in today's world. How do we translate and interpret these teachings without losing the essential and often intangible blessings of traditional methods? How do we teach something that really helps people? Each teacher must come to his or her own conclusions, and the answers seem to run the gamut from very conservative to highly experimental. Although the nature of mind transcends time and culture, the psyche is influenced by cultural history and language, so we must address these differences to be effective in a global context. After all, Buddhism changed as it went from India to Tibet, Japan, Korea, Burma, Thailand, Sri Lanka, and China, and it will continue to change as it goes out to the rest of the world.

My goal is to present you with something of the essence of Machig's teachings, based on what has been effective in my own experience as a Buddhist practitioner, a woman, and a teacher. This exposure may provide you with a doorway to pursuing more traditional training in Chöd, or it may stand on its own as a method to help you work with the challenges of your life. In either event, I believe Machig's approach of engaging and feeding the "enemy" provides a revolutionary paradigm shift from domination to tolerance and integration. Religious systems that set up battlegrounds internally and externally have brought us a polarized experience both within ourselves and in our ever more fright-ening world. No matter how many demons we try to destroy, more appear in their place; no matter how many terrorists we kill, more fill their ranks. In order to be effective we need a new model, based on compassion, inclusion, and dialogue. This approach has incredible implications, personally and collectively. Although we will focus primarily on the personal, in the last part of the book I will also touch on the collective applications of Machig Labdrön's teachings, which humankind so urgently needs in our divided world.

Having spent my life bridging East and West, I am deeply committed to both ensuring that the tradition of Tibetan Bud-dhism reaches the West intact *and* adapting those teachings to Western life today. I myself have continued to strictly follow the traditional teachings in my training with Tibetan lamas. But when I teach I have found it effective both to transmit the traditional teachings and to use methods that have made the teachings practical in my life as a Westerner. I believe that deem-phasizing the culturally specific aspects of this ancient wisdom will make it more accessible and will benefit many who might be put off by the complexity of the Tibetan tradition.

Therefore in this book I will not be attempting to teach Chöd in its original form, since that practice requires in-person trans-mission from a qualified teacher, uses a bell, thighbone trumpet, and drum, and is sung in Tibetan. My focus will be on using the principles of the practice as a springboard for something applica-ble in modern life, something useful in relieving suffering and bringing the average person closer to inner freedom.

INTRODUCTION

My intention is that this book will communicate something of the great wisdom of my teachers and give you a living link with the teachings of Machig Labdrön. May it prove useful in your life, may it effectively help to liberate your demons, and may it ultimately contribute to the creation of a more peaceful world.

PART ONE

THE ANCIENT PRACTICE

1

MEETING THE DEMON

The malignant male and female demons
Who create myriad troubles and obstructions
Seem real before one has reached enlightenment.
But when one realizes their true nature,
They become Protectors,
And through their help and assistance
One attains numerous accomplishments.

—*Tibet's great yogi Milarepa (1052–1135)*

MAHATMA GANDHI, one of the greatest peace activists of the twentieth century, changed the course of India's history by quite literally feeding his enemy. Gandhi, the story goes, was told that he would be visited by a British official who would threaten him with prison if he did not give up what the British considered to be the subversive activity of marching in protest of the British salt tax. Gandhi's advisers suggested putting nails in the road to puncture the tires of the official's car.

"You will do nothing of the sort," said Gandhi. "We shall invite him to tea."

Crestfallen, his followers obeyed. When the official arrived, he entered full of pomp and purpose. "Now then, Mr. Gandhi, this so-called salt marching has to stop at once. Otherwise I shall be forced to arrest you."

"Well," said Gandhi, "first, let's have some tea."

The Englishman agreed, reluctantly. Then, when he had drained his cup, he said briskly, "Now we must get down to business. About these marches . . ."

Gandhi smiled. "Not just yet. Have some more tea and biscuits; there are more important things to talk about."

And so it went. The Englishman became increasingly interested in what the Mahatma had to say, drank many more cups of tea and ate many more biscuits until he was completely diverted from his official task, and eventually went away won over to Gandhi's cause. Gandhi used the medium of tea, an English ritual that implies civility and mutual respect, and literally fed this enemy until he became an ally. His tactic of feeding rather than fighting contributed to one of the most extraordinary nonviolent revolutions in history.

This same tactic had been used nearly a millennium earlier, when the great eleventh-century Tibetan yogini Machig Labdrön was receiving initiation from her teacher, Sonam Lama, with several of her spiritual sisters. At a key moment in the initiation, Machig magically rose up from where she was sitting until she was suspended in the air about a foot from the ground, and there she danced and spoke in Sanskrit. In a state of profound meditation she passed through the clay walls of the temple unimpeded and flew into a tree above a small pond outside the monastery.

The pond was the residence of a powerful *naga,* or water spirit. These capricious, mythic beings are believed to cause disruption and disease when disturbed, and can also act as treasure holders or protectors when they are propitiated. This particular naga was so terrifying that the local people did not even dare to look at the pond, never mind approach it. But Machig landed in the tree above the pond and stayed there in a state of meditation.

The water spirit considered young Machig's arrival to be a direct confrontation. He approached her threateningly, but she remained in meditation, unafraid. This infuriated him, so he gathered a huge army of nagas from the region in an attempt to overwhelm her. When she saw this mass of terrifying magical apparitions coming, Machig instantly transformed her body into a food offering, and as her biography (found in my book *Women of Wisdom*) states: "They could not devour her because she was egoless."

Not only did the aggression of the nagas evaporate, but they committed themselves to Machig, promising not to harm her or other beings, vowing to protect her, and pledging to serve her and anyone who followed her teachings. By meeting the demons and offering her body as food to them with unshakable compassion rather than fighting against them, Machig turned the demons into allies.

While studying Machig's teachings, I began to think about the Western understanding of demons. When I looked up the word in an English dictionary, I discovered that "demon" has not always had such a bad reputation. Derived from the Greek *daemon* or *daimon*, the term originally referred to a person's guiding spirit. The Greek daemon was a divine creature, a guiding spirit to be trusted and relied upon. This early belief in the daemon gradually changed with the advent of the Christian attack on pagan beliefs, so that by the Middle Ages demons were being blamed for every possible disaster, despised and feared as evil. We will see that through the process of meeting and feeding a demon with love and compassion, it can be transformed into a daemon. In this way your demons become your allies, just as the fearsome nagas transformed into protectors when Machig offered them her body as food.

Tales from Western mythology stand in stark contrast to the stories of Machig and Gandhi. The myth of the twelve labors of Hercules is a classic of Western literature, a shining example of the conquering hero's quest, one of the most important personal and political myths to guide Western culture. To absolve himself of the murders of his children, Hercules is given twelve tasks, the second of which sends him to Lake Lerna in southern Italy, where a nine-headed, many-legged serpent called Hydra has been attacking innocent passersby. Hercules arrives at the lake accompanied by his nephew and pupil, Iolaus. Upon finding the lair of Hydra, the two men shoot flaming arrows to draw out the beast. But when Hydra emerges and Hercules wades into the water, the angry Hydra wraps its leg around Hercules' ankle, trapping him, and its assistant, a giant crab, drags him to the edge of a bottomless lake. To Hercules' dismay, every time he severs one of Hydra's heads, two grow back in its place.

Ensnared by the monster, Hercules calls to Iolaus for help. Rushing to his uncle's aid, the young man uses a burning branch to cauterize the stub of each of the heads Hercules chops off, preventing the Hydra from growing more. This gives Hercules the upper hand, and eventually only one head remains. This head is immortal, but Hercules realizes he can cut through the mortal neck that supports it. He chops the head off, but it still lies before him, hissing and staring. So he buries the immortal head under a boulder, considering the monster vanquished and his second task completed.

But what kind of victory has Hercules achieved? Has he actually eliminated the enemy or merely suppressed it? Hydra's immortal head, the governing force of its constellated energy, is still seething under the boulder and could reemerge if circumstances permitted. What does this say about Hercules' accomplishment, and, more generally, about the monster-slaying heroic mentality that so enthralls and permeates Western literature and society?

Various versions of the myth of the dragon-slaying hero have dominated the Western psyche over the last forty-five hundred years. Although the positive aspect of the myth can lead to heroic battles against truly dangerous demons like Hitler, as well as against disease, poverty, and hunger, it also poses terrible dangers. Among these is inflation of those who identify themselves with the role of the dragon-slaying hero, regardless of their virtue. Another is projecting evil onto our opponents, demonizing them, and justifying their murder, while we claim to be wholly identified with good. The tendency to kill rather than to engage the dragon prevents us from knowing our own demons, and from turning them into allies.

Evidence that we continue to live out this myth can be seen

everywhere, from popular movies to current global events. In today's battles each side identifies itself with the divine good as it struggles against evil. The polarization of good and evil justifies violence as a necessary sacrifice that must be endured to attain victory. Today perhaps more than ever before, we are trapped by overidentification with the dragon-slaying myth.

Our state of polarization is not only in the outer world; within ourselves we fight demons of addiction, stress, trauma, anger, and self-hatred, to name just a few. We try to dominate everything, inside ourselves and without, including Mother Nature herself. But rather than ever achieving final victory, we become engulfed by the struggle, which holds us captive. As we seek to kill the dragon, we find ourselves in danger of destroying each other and the natural world, making human life on this planet untenable.

We can see signs of the ineffectiveness of this myth at every turn. For example:

• Americans spend tens of billions of dollars every year on products and programs to try to lose weight, yet the "battle of the bulge" remains a lost cause. Chronic dieters frequently add five to ten pounds to their weight every time they diet, and eating disorders triggered by the starve-and-binge cycles of diets are killing thousands of us every year.

• Our pursuit of such things as wealth and success is so defined by struggle that even if we finally reach these goals, the ingrained pattern of striving won't allow us to enjoy the fruits of our labor. And once we succeed, we face a draining, never-ending battle to defend what we've gained.

- Experts in addiction tell us that using willpower to fight addiction does not lead to sobriety, and we must stop thinking we can overcome addiction by struggling against it.

- We do not try to understand our illnesses. Instead, whenever we get sick we immediately begin to develop strategies to "fight" the illness. Obituary columns routinely read: "So-and-so died after a long *battle* with cancer."

- Religious fundamentalism is growing in many countries around the world today, emphasizing the chasm between good and evil. Each group staunchly believes it has God on its side. By identifying our own religion with good and others with evil, we are locked in an endless struggle and never get around to facing the evil in ourselves or in our own political systems.

- We have raped the natural world, damming rivers and carelessly using up resources, polluting the atmosphere, and battling the nurturer, Mother Earth. Now nature fights back with a fury of natural disasters: hurricanes, tsunamis, tornadoes, droughts, floods, and global warming. In response we fight climate change, seeking to stop it without addressing the underlying attitude that created the problem to begin with.

- We try to eliminate enemies through war and violence, but violence breeds more violence. For example, a study by U.S. intelligence agencies showed that rather than stemming the growth of terrorism, the war in Iraq had invigorated radicalism and worsened the global terrorism threat.

As we live by the myth in which we seek out, battle against, and ultimately destroy the enemy within and without, we also teach this myth to our children. We see this theme in fairy tales, religious stories, and political rhetoric, where heroes like Saint George kill the dragon or vanquish the hidden monster, often with a powerless maiden being "saved" by the hero. We also see it endlessly in films and television programs. Seeking out and destroying "the enemy" may look like the best solution, but in actuality it's creating a more and more dangerous world. Clearly we need to explore the alternative of engaging and communicating with the enemy rather than destroying it.

In this book we focus primarily on personal demons, cycling back to collective and political demons at the end. This is because the personal is at the root of our global demons, and by working with our own demons we create a shift that ripples out into the world. The approach of feeding rather than fighting our demons provides a way to *pay attention* to the demons within us, avoiding the dangers of repressing what we fear inside ourselves. Facing and feeding our demons avoids the creation of a raging monster that wreaks destruction both in us and in the world.

I propose that we follow Machig's example: the dragon is not slain or even fought against, but drawn out and fearlessly nurtured. In this way we bridge the schism between "good" and "evil" and the potential enemy is transformed into an ally. This means that the energy that has been tied up in struggle becomes a positive and potentially protective force, a daemon rather than a demon. Every battle that we have within ourselves is tying up resources that could be put to far better use.

In mythology the dragon often guards a secret treasure. Through feeding our demons and transforming them into allies, we discover our own treasures that have been hidden by our pre-occupation with doing battle. As it turns out, when liberated, the energy of the demon that has been locked in struggle *is* the treasure. Feeding our demons also makes us less of a threat in the world. When we become aware of our demons and offer them an elixir of conscious acceptance and compassion, we are much less likely to project them onto others.

Carl G. Jung, the famous Swiss psychologist, described our dark side as "the shadow," which might emerge in dreams or be projected onto others. The shadow he described consists of those parts of ourselves that the conscious mind deems unacceptable. The shadow is the repressed self, the unwelcome aspects of our personality we disown. It might be our shame, our anger, or our prejudices. It is that which we don't want others to know about us, and it often appears in dreams doing things our conscious self would not consider. When a married person dreams of having an affair, this is the shadow. We are often unaware of the shadow parts of our personality, because they are unseen by the conscious mind. The shadow encourages us to finish the whole plate of cookies when we intend not to eat any. The shadow blurts out an insult to someone we are trying to impress.

The process of feeding our demons is a method for bringing our shadow into consciousness and accessing the treasures it holds rather than repressing it. If the shadow is not made conscious and integrated, it operates undercover, becoming the saboteur of our best intentions as well as causing harm to others. Bringing the shadow to awareness reduces its destructive power and releases the life energy stored in it. By befriending that which scares us most, we find our own wisdom. This resolution of inner conflict also lessens the evil produced by the unconscious that contributes to dangerous collective movements.

In the practice of feeding our demons, we offer what is most precious (our own body) to that which is most threatening and frightening (our demons), and in doing so we overcome the root of all suffering, which in Buddhist terms is egocentricity. To give you an idea of how feeding your demons might look in a real-life situation, let me tell you a story of what happened some years ago while I was traveling in Tibet.

My friend Sara and I were traveling by bus on a pilgrimage. By this time I had come to a personal understanding of demons, was teaching the practice of Chöd, and had developed the method of feeding your demons that I describe in this book. One day we moved to a significantly higher altitude, having driven throughout the night. We had eaten one too many cans of mackerel in tomato sauce as the bus bounced interminably over the dirt track, aggravating our altitude headaches. The dust was so thick that even wrapping my head in a scarf didn't keep it out.

Sara was sitting alone, crying, on a seat ahead of me. I went and sat next to her. She told me about the depression that was attacking her, a demon that she had been battling all her life, having grown up in a family where she was unwanted. She was desperate, convulsing in sobs. Attempting to help her feed this demon seemed like the best thing I could offer her, even under these difficult circumstances, where I couldn't go through the steps as completely as I normally would. So right there, lurching along on the dusty road, we began the process.

I said, "Okay, Sara, let's try an experiment. Let's see what it would look like if you were to give this pain a form."

She closed her eyes and brought her awareness into her body, finding a sensation of nausea and grief she described as dark, reddish purple, heavy, and thick. Then I suggested she allow this to take a living form in front of her. She saw a huge purple monster with a gaping mouth where its stomach should have been. It wanted to consume her.

I said, "Let's see if we can find the real need that lies behind what this demon says it wants."

Sara asked the demon what it needed, and it said it needed her to stop trying to escape, that if she did that, it would feel love and acceptance. Then I suggested that Sara visualize dissolving her body into a nectar of love and feeding the demon until it was completely satisfied.

Slowly Sara stopped sobbing and became quiet. After a while she said, "I fed it, and it got smaller and smaller. I don't understand how it happened, but it's gone."

After enjoying the moment she said, "My mind has relaxed into a peaceful space I never thought was possible for me. But I still don't know how it happened."

Several months after we returned home, Sara wrote me a letter about this experience. She said, "This trip was the most difficult physical and emotional thing I'd ever done. By nature I am a loner. To be in a large group was difficult, especially since you were the only person I knew before I left on the pilgrimage. That day on the bus when I broke down, I'd reached a point in my life where if I couldn't live with myself, I was going to die. Literally.

That day all the pain came together. The pain in my head caused by the altitude. The pain in my heart caused by my terrible childhood traumas. The pain of all that I was seeing in Tibet. The pain was too much. When I fed this demon of pain and sadness, it was as if I'd come out the other side as someone completely new. I felt somehow reborn."

The interesting thing about Sara's experience was that it wasn't just a momentary shift. In her letter she said that the pain she had carried all her life never came back. Of course feeding your demons doesn't always liberate you from long-held pain in one session; usually that requires a series of encounters, but in Sara's case, one was all it took.

In considering the stories of Gandhi, Machig, and Sara, we see a compelling alternative to Hercules' solution of battling against demons. Inspired by their compassion and fearlessness, we can now take a look at how we might meet our demons, feed them, and perhaps even turn them into allies—untapped sources of support and protection.

2

DISCOVERING THE PRACTICE

At first a yogi feels his mind
Is tumbling like a waterfall;
In midcourse, like the Ganges,
It flows on slow and gentle;
In the end, it is a great
Vast ocean, where the lights
Of child and mother merge in one.

— *The Song of Tilopa (988–1069)*

I SHALL NEVER FORGET the first time I witnessed the Chöd practice. It was 1973, I was twenty-five, and I had recently returned to India to be with my Tibetan teachers following a year in the United States. After three and a half years as a Tibetan Buddhist nun, I was in a state of great transition. Although I had been happy as a nun, at twenty-five I decided I wanted to follow my spiritual path without the shaved head, robes, and vows that separated me from people in the West.

I had given back my vows to a kind, highly respected lama, who did not chastise me, but rather suggested I dedicate to all beings the merit gained by my time as a monastic. He also suggested I perform certain purification practices to clear any obstacles that might come from breaking my commitments. I began the practices he suggested while I was living in a cabin in the foothills of the Himalayas in an area called Kulu Valley, near the town of Manali, where my meditation master, Apho Rinpoche, a married lama, lived with his wife and four children and a group of monks, nuns, and yogis. Manali was the last stop before the Rohtang Pass, gateway to the Himalayan kingdom of Lahaul. A latticework of mud streets and wooden stalls extended away from the main road, which could be identified by the tea shops, hardware stores, restaurants, food stalls, and cloth vendors that ran along it. There were no hotels and one battered storefront post office. A couple of miles upriver, on a steep hillside, was Apho Rinpoche's place (Rinpoche is a title of respect given to a Tibetan Buddhist spiritual master).

The people from Manali looked like they'd stepped out of a fairy tale. The women wore hand-woven blankets held together by a belt and a huge safety pin at the shoulder. Bright cherry-red cotton scarves, tied under their hair in the back, covered their heads. The men wore handmade shoes and thin cotton trousers with matching knee-length tunics, belted with thick layers of raw felt rope. Kulu Valley produced red rice, apples, and plums as cash crops, and its people lived on this income and subsistence farming.

I was renting a small house close to Apho Rinpoche's home. My house, characteristic of many in Manali, had covered porches around it so you could sit outside protected from the weather. From my front porch I could see across the river to the orchards on the other side. Above them, conifer forests gave way to the glistening snowy peaks of the Himalayas.

One afternoon as I was sitting in my cabin after lunch, I heard joyful singing from the hill on the other side of the stream. A storm was gathering, and low dark clouds were blowing down the valley from the Rohtang Pass. Wind whipped up the chartreuse hillside across from the cascading stream below my cabin. There on the hill I saw a girl of about fourteen wearing a traditional pink blanket dress. Unaware of me, she was dancing and singing at the top of her lungs, twirling among the cows she was tending.

Shortly after this I went down the path through the apple orchard to Apho Rinpoche's home to ask him some questions about my meditation practice. I arrived at Rinpoche's stone house just moments before the monsoon storm broke. Rinpoche sat upstairs in the corner room overlooking the courtyard in front of his house and the hillside beyond. He had recently settled his family in Manali after escaping from Tibet. He was in his fifties and still handsome, with a thin mustache, short gray hair, and a big smile with beautiful, even white teeth. He wore several layers of faded cotton shirts in various shades of red and orange over a full-length brown robe tied at the waist with a woven belt of red silk. He sat cross-legged on his bed, leaning on pillows against the wall. Perpendicular to his bed was a lower bed covered with a carpet.

On the table alongside his bed was a delicate Tibetan teacup on a silver stand with a silver cover to keep the tea hot during long conversations. Next to the cup were a light blue Chinese thermos and a couple of Tibetan texts, their foot-long loose folios lying on top of cloth wrappings. On one wall was a cupboard containing his shrine. He gestured for me to sit on the lower bed. Against the opposite wall was a carpet, where a Tibetan man was sitting.

The man visiting Rinpoche was a refugee road worker. He wore tattered wool pants and a gray shirt with several buttons missing, and he looked pale and thin—almost haunted. He was talking to Rinpoche about his poor health, asking for help. As the rain drummed down outside, the three of us sat there together drinking sweet tea poured from the Chinese thermos by Rinpoche's wife, Urgyen Chödrön, whom we called Amala. Rinpoche listened, nodding and making sympathetic noises, looking concerned. Eventually he told the man to come back that night, and he suggested that I also come back that evening.

I have always wondered if he had some foreknowledge of my connection with the ceremony that would occur. In any case, that night I took my rattling Chinese flashlight and slid down the muddy path from my house in the dark with rain still pounding down. As I walked into Rinpoche's darkened house, I could hear the rhythmic sound of drums and bells. Climbing the dark staircase at the end of the hallway, I saw light under the curtain of the altar room.

Inside was a group of maroon-robed monks and nuns arranged in a circle around the Tibetan man, who was lying on his back with his eyes closed, motionless. All of the monks and nuns held a Tibetan bell in the left hand, and in the right hand a drum that they were turning from side to side. They were singing together, in a state of deep concentration. I quietly took a seat behind the circle and listened to the melody that rose and fell, punctuated by a thighbone trumpet, the rhythm carried by the bells and double-faced drums. Sitting at the edge of their circle in the dim light, I felt profound longing for something I couldn't name. Was it a memory, or was it a call to something new?

After the practice was over, the road worker got up, shook himself, and smiled softly. He quietly made offerings to the monks and nuns and departed into the stormy night. As I climbed back up the hill to my cabin, I thought about the storm and the young girl dancing and singing that afternoon, and I felt her presence had signaled something about to break open in my life. I knew this practice called me home. I went to bed that night in my old cotton flowered sleeping bag to the sound of rain pounding on the tin roof of my cabin and the beat of the drum in my heart.

The next afternoon I was sitting with Rinpoche having tea when the road worker came back. The man was transformed. He looked radiant, healthy, and had a sparkle in his eyes that hadn't been there the day before. He thanked Rinpoche and we drank tea together.

After he left I asked Rinpoche, "What was that practice last night?"

And he said, "That's the practice of Chöd."

I knew a little about the practice from a book on Tibetan yoga and meditation I had read, and asked if I could learn the Chöd. He nodded immediately, as though he'd been expecting the question, and said I could begin to learn it from Gegyen Khyentse, an accomplished old monk who served as the instructor for the monks and nuns at Rinpoche's center. Performing the traditional practice meant learning to use the double-sided drum in the right hand, the bell in the left, and occasionally the thigh-bone trumpet. Apho Rinpoche's wife, Amala, kindly lent me her drum to practice with. I began to learn sitting on my porch every afternoon with Gegyen and Paul, a Dutchman whom I had known before in Holland. He had been studying with Apho Rinpoche and other lamas since I had first met him four years earlier in Holland, right before he left for India and I returned to Nepal and was ordained by the Karmapa.

The Chöd drum has two strikers made of tightly rolled balls of cloth or beads wrapped in cloth. They hang down from strings on either side of the double-faced drum, which is about a foot in diameter. When the drum is held up vertically and turned with a strong wrist movement, the strikers hit opposite sides at the same time. Gegyen explained that this drum symbolized the insepara-bility of cyclic existence and nirvana, hopes and fears, gods and demons.

The strings of my strikers were always getting tangled, and I despaired of ever becoming competent. Gegyen would just laugh and say, "Let's try it again." My arm ached, and I blamed my drum for misbehaving, but I persevered, finally getting the hang of it. Gradually I added the bell in my left hand. Doing both simulta-neously was like trying to pat my head and rub my stomach at the same time. Gegyen taught us that the sound of the bell was the sound of emptiness and represented feminine wisdom. Leaning back and squinting so that his eyes practically disappeared, he said, "All that appears as solid is merely appearing and has no essential nature. What we think of as real is like the places and people we see in dreams." Then he laughed, grinning toothlessly, and looked at us, nodding. "Okay, let's do it again."

This time of learning Chöd brought the blossoming of a romance with Paul, my Dutch friend, that had been kindling during a four-year correspondence while I was a nun. Soon we entered a relationship, and my solo time was over. I had a yearning to understand this practice more deeply, and I decided I would pursue it as soon as I could. But by the end of that spring we realized I was pregnant, and we decided to return to the United States, via Holland. We married in Delhi and then, after visiting my parents in New Hampshire, we settled in a primitive berry-picker's cottage on Vashon Island, near Seattle, where we began a small Buddhist meditation center. Over the next few years I gave birth to two daughters only seventeen months apart. Most of the time, my Chöd drum hung on the wall gathering dust as I coped with the sudden change from a quiet monastic life to sleepless nights caring for two beautiful, active baby girls, Sherab and Aloka.

After four years my marriage dissolved amicably. Then two years later I married an Italian documentary filmmaker and moved to Italy. In 1980 I gave birth to twins in Rome. They were born a little early, but both were over five pounds, and after three weeks in the hospital they were able to come home. We named the boy Costanzo (Cos for short) and the girl Chiara. At this point I had four children under six. I had my hands full, but we began to find a rhythm in our lives, and things seemed to be settling in a good way.

Then, early in the morning of June 1, 1980, I pulled myself

out from under the covers and shuffled through the bathroom into a small adjacent room to check the twins. Little Cos was awake and gurgling. I kissed him, changed his diaper, and took him in my arms to nurse him, letting his sister, Chiara, continue to sleep in her little blue crib. I was relieved at not having them both awake and needing to be fed at the same time.

My breasts were huge and heavy with milk, and my back was aching as I sat nursing Cos. I looked at Chiara in her little bed nearby. She was sleeping on her stomach, her preferred position, but she was too quiet. I put Cos down in his bed and moved toward Chiara's crib. Looking down on her, I could tell she wasn't breathing. A cold wind rushed through me as I bent to pick her up. She was lying with her head turned to the side. Her face was slightly purple around the eyes, and a trickle of dried blood came from her nose.

Her body had a slightly stiff quality and seemed lighter than it should. I screamed for my husband. He ran in, and I told him Chiara was dead. He took her out of my hands, moaning, "No, no, no," trying futilely to get her to breathe.

I knew Chiara was gone, but we all rushed to the hospital in the hope that she could be brought back. As we drove through the early spring morning on the narrow road, I thought, "This is something that can't be reversed, can't be fixed. Everything is shifting, and I can't do anything to stop it." My future had become blurry, like rain falling on an unfinished watercolor.

I became oddly calm. I felt like I was floating out of the car, noticing irrelevant details—buds opening, a cat scampering into a hedge. Then a rush of emotions surged through me. Grief, fear, guilt, and pain-laced memories of Chiara, her tiny white body, her sweet-smelling skin, and her darling smile. Was her death my fault? Could I have done something to prevent it? Chiara had always been paler, smaller than her brother. She had seemed to be half in another world. I had always felt there was something not right with her, but the pediatrician had assured me she was fine.

Now I sat in the front seat of the car holding her wrapped in the checked quilt I had made for her. Sherab and Aloka were in the backseat with baby Cos, crying and calling for Chiara, which means "clarity" in Italian. What I needed more than anything at that moment was clarity. I felt broken.

The young doctor who met us at the Velletri Hospital was dark-haired and smoking a cigarette. He took us into an examining room and casually pronounced Chiara dead. "*È morta.*" She had died of sudden infant death syndrome (SIDS), sometimes called crib death. The doctor said this kind of death was common; they had already had several babies die the same way in the past few months. There was no known cause. It just happened: every mother's greatest fear.

After Chiara's death I spiraled into depression. I questioned everything: my marriage, the path I had been following, and all the choices I had made up to that point in my life. Everything hurt, and I felt lost. I was plagued by demons of guilt, even though I was told I wasn't to blame. As I groped for some anchor, some hope in this darkness, I developed an acute need to know the stories of Buddhist women. All the Buddhist literature that I had studied was about enlightened men, their lives, and their stories. As a mother with three small children, sitting in a pool of sadness, I needed the stories of women. What did *they* do when they reached crossroads like these in their lives? I knew the founder of the Chöd practice, Machig Labdrön, was a woman, but I didn't know much about her, so I decided to research her life and the lives of women teachers from Tibet, hoping to find some answers for my own life.

That summer we were at a retreat with Namkhai Norbu Rinpoche, a Tibetan lama who lived in Italy. I remember sitting outside on a platform as he led us in the practice of Chöd. Part of the practice is visualizing Machig Labdrön as a youthful white dakini (the female embodiment of wisdom). Normally we would do Chöd once, but that night he kept repeating it again and again. It was well past midnight when instead of seeing a young dakini, I had a vision of an old woman emerging from a charnel ground. She had gray hair streaming from her head. She was naked, with long, pendulous breasts, and her skin was a dark golden brown. She stopped right in front of me and looked at me intensely with both challenge and compassion; she remained there for the rest of the invocation, and afterward I felt a fundamental shift.

That night I had a dream in which I was trying to get to a hill in Kathmandu called Swayambhu, which actually means "self-realization." It's the site of a very well known temple and stupa (a white dome structure containing many relics) in Kathmandu Valley, and I had lived there in my early days as a nun. I had a series of repetitive dreams, with slight variations, every night for a week. I dreamed that I must go to Swayambhu, but there were many obstacles, including war.

After these dreams I decided to travel to Nepal in search of the story of women lamas. Leaving my children and husband behind, I made the long journey to Nepal. On my arrival I left my luggage at my hotel and walked slowly up the long staircase that took me to the top of the hill where the Swayambhu temple is. When I reached the last step, there was Gyalwa, a monk who had been my dear friend when I had first gone to Nepal at age nineteen and my closest friend when I lived there in a tiny room as a nun. He was standing at the top of the stairs as if he had been waiting for me, the wrinkles at the corners of his eyes deepening in a smile. He greeted me and took me to his room in the monastery down a narrow staircase spattered with Tibetan butter tea.

Gyalwa poured me a cup of butter tea and offered me deep-fried *kapsi*, a stale cracker made at the Tibetan New Year. As I drank the steaming cup of tea from a wooden cup and gnawed on the kapsi, I told him in Tibetan about the loss of Chiara and my search for the stories of great Tibetan women teachers. He tapped his foot, then his eyes lit up and he stood up on his bed. From high on his shelf he pulled down a big, thick Tibetan text and said, "This is the biography of Machig Labdrön." Goose bumps covered my arms as he handed me the orange cloth-covered folios and I looked through them. I asked if we could translate her biography together, and he said, "Yes, come back in a few days."

The whole text was called *An Exposition of Transforming the Aggregates into an Offering of Food, Illuminating the Meaning of Chöd,* and the first two chapters were entitled "The Marvelous Life of Machig Labdrön," by Namkha Gyaltsen, who lived in the fourteenth century. As I sat with another monk who knew English and the resident lama, translating Machig's story day after day, page after page, I felt I was finding a thread that would lead me out of my confusion. I learned that Machig taught that we should feed, not fight, our demons; although I did not yet understand how this would apply to my own life, the seeds of her teachings were planted.

From that moment on, Machig became a beacon in my search for wisdom in a challenging world, a vision of female potential. Her life story and the teachings of Chöd were a key to digging myself out from the darkness I had fallen into. I began to understand the nature of demons and the need to feed them. I learned that Machig had been a child prodigy in Tibet during the eleventh century, the time of a great renaissance of Buddhism there. She lived as a nun in her youth, becoming a renowned reader of the Sutra (teachings of the Buddha) of the Perfection of Wisdom — the Prajnaparamita Sutra — in the homes of her teacher's patrons. The reading of the sutra was thought to bless homes and bring good fortune to the family.

As she grew up, Machig received teachings from both Indian and Tibetan sages, and she had many profound experiences, including the occasion when she offered her body as food to the attacking army of nagas. When she was in her twenties, she left monastic life to live with an accomplished Indian yogi, Topabhadra, and they had three children. After having been held in high esteem, she was now criticized for becoming a "fallen" nun, and the family had to move to another area of Tibet. Following several years of living with Topabhadra and being a mother, she then felt the call to return to her teachers and deepen her practice. So she left her children with their father and returned to the life of a wandering yogini. During a retreat in a mountain cave, she received teachings directly from the female Buddha, Tara, and gradually developed her own teachings on offering the body to feed the demons. This resulted in her most famous teaching: the Chöd.

By the time she was forty, Machig's teachings had spread all over Tibet, and word of her wisdom reached India. The Buddhist patriarchs there heard that a woman was claiming to have a Buddhist teaching that originated in Tibet, not in India. This was especially surprising because, at the time, Buddhist theology flowed exclusively from India to Tibet, not the other way around. As a result she caused quite a stir among the high-ups in Indian Buddhism. They sent a delegation of scholars to Tibet to challenge her, but when she emerged from these debates victorious, her fame spread even more widely. She not only manifested great scholarly knowledge, but showed true insight into the nature of mind and was a great healer. Her children became her disciples, and along with others they eventually became her lineage holders. Her teachings became the only Buddhist lineage in Tibet originated by a woman.

Machig's story and the five biographies of female Tibetan mystics that I subsequently found became the subject of my first book, *Women of Wisdom*. In the confusion following Chiara's death, discovering these biographies felt like finding tracks in a vast snow-covered landscape. Following these tracks, I began to find my way.

3

WHAT ARE DEMONS?

With a loving mind, cherish more than a child
The hostile gods and demons of apparent existence,
And tenderly surround yourself with them.

—*Machig Labdrön (1055–1145)*

IN 1985, twelve years after I had first learned Chöd from Ge-gyen in Manali, something happened that made the practice sud-denly relevant to my personal life. I had been living in Italy for six years, five of which had passed since Chiara's death, and I had come to realize that my marriage was never going to work because of my husband's repeated infidelities and issues related to his ad-dictions. During the separation leading up to our divorce, I dis-covered the power of Chöd in a very intimate way. The divorce proceedings had come to an impasse over the issue of custody of our son. According to Italian law, our son, Cos, the surviving twin, could stay in Italy, or I could stay in Italy with him, but I could not leave with Cos without his father's permission, which he refused to give. This was a source of great tension between us, and it seemed we could find no resolution. We were due to go to court soon when one night I thought, "I'm just going to do the Chöd practice with this situation in mind."

As the children slept in their beds, I picked up my drum and bell and began to sing the ancient melody of the Chöd practice. During the practice you transform your own body into nectar that feeds all beings, starting with the Buddhas and enlightened ones. This nectar is offered with compassion to many kinds of guests, including personified forms of your demons, such as fear. I saw my husband as one of the guests, and I personified my fear of him. As I imagined dissolving my own body into nectar of love and acceptance, I visualized that he was able to drink all that he needed of this nectar. In making this offering, I temporarily released my anger and my desire to get away from him with our son, and offered him this elixir with compassion. Temporarily, I let go of my end of our tug-of-war.

I also fed a personified form of my fear demon, which I saw as a haunted blue figure with a terrible grimace, spiky hair, and suction-cup hands like octopus tentacles. By nourishing both my husband and the fear demon with open generosity, I relaxed my struggle against them. After both were satisfied and I had completed the rest of the practice, I felt free of "me against you" tension, and I went to bed feeling more peaceful and relaxed than I had for months.

The next day my husband called from the apartment he was renting on the other side of Rome and asked if we could talk. I'll never forget that meeting. We were sitting there on the beige cotton couch in the living room we had once shared. The windows were open and the morning sun was streaming in.

He said, "Last night something changed for me. This morning I decided I should let you go back to the States with Cos. I understand that I have been unfair and that you have suffered a lot. I trust that you will facilitate my relationship with Cos, and will help to make me as much a part of his life as possible."

I looked at him in shock and disbelief. This was a complete reversal of his previous stance. What had happened? And then I remembered the Chöd practice I had done the night before, when I had let go of the battle I had been fighting for months and fed him with compassion, and fed my own demon of fear with love as well. It was as though by releasing my end of the cord in our tug-of-war, the tension was no longer there for him either, allowing him space to change his mind.

Through this very concrete experience I saw for the first time that this practice of feeding demons was something that related specifically and directly to my life, to my struggles as a Western woman and as a mother. I realized that the demons that I was feeding in the Chöd were actually very much a part of my own day-to-day life; they were my "stuff," my issues, my fears, my anger. They were not Tibetan; they were not exotic demons from an Asian scroll painting that had no direct relationship to my ordinary life. Suddenly this practice seemed completely relevant in addressing my hopes and fears.

After this experience, my understanding of the Chöd practice changed, and I began to personify and feed my demons whether they were emotions, illnesses, or fears. It was a bit later, when I began to teach the Chöd, that I developed a version of the five-step practice you will find here, but at this point my fundamental understanding of my demons as the inner conflicts in my life was formed. Whatever was coming up for me I fed in the

Chöd practice. It was easy to find the demons. I carried them with me all the time! And no matter what demon I brought to the feast, the result was always freedom from tension.

In 1989, three years after I moved back to the States, I met my current husband, David. He was my daughter's theater and dance teacher. Meeting him triggered the appearance of a big demon for me, an abandonment demon exacerbated by the infidelities of my Italian husband. As a result of this demon I would sometimes destroy a promising relationship by wanting commitment too soon, or I would provoke betrayal as a kind of self-fulfilling prophecy.

I would think, "I don't want to have anything to do with this ridiculous, humiliating fear of abandonment. If I ignore it, it will go away. Besides, I have good reasons to feel like I'm going to be abandoned." But the abandonment demon did not go away; it got stronger and more persistent. I finally began feeding my abandonment demon in Chöd practice, because I realized that until I started taking care of it, it was going to raise hell with my relationship with Dave. I had fought against this demon for years, but that didn't mean I had been truly paying attention to it.

I decided to experiment by working with my abandonment demon intensely—every day for a month—using a journal to keep track of what happened. As well as doing the Chöd, I adopted a Western psychological approach by embodying and personifying my abandonment demon and communicating with it, changing places and becoming it, and offering it what it needed. I created a simple version of the five steps based on the principles of Chöd: dissolving my body into nectar and feeding it to the demon until it was completely satisfied, at which point it either dissolved or changed into a positive figure. At the end of this process I rested in the space of awareness that opened up after the demon was satisfied and dissolved.

When I first located my abandonment demon, she was a child of about five, with pathetic, shifty eyes. She had messy brown hair and big blue eyes, but she had the pointed teeth of a vampire. She said, "He's going to leave. Listen to me; you know I'm right. You know it's always going to come down to you and me. I'm the only real friend you have. I'll always be here, telling you the truth about what's going to happen. I'm predictable. At least you can count on me." As she was saying this, she seemed to be getting stronger.

As the days went by, I fed her on a regular basis using Chöd and the method I'd developed, and she began to change. Eventually when I called her up before me to feed her, she was no longer a vampire. She just looked sad. By the end of the month she looked vulnerable and loving, grateful for the attention I was giving her. The amazing thing was that after this concerted effort, she actually stopped causing trouble in my life and no longer bothered me. I had accepted that she would always be with me as my "core issue," but that didn't turn out to be the case. On a practical level, things changed too. My relationship with Dave improved, and eventually we developed the wonderful marriage we have today.

Around this time, encouraged by my teacher Namkhai Norbu Rinpoche, I began teaching Chöd retreats. As I did so, I saw that the practice of feeding demons was difficult for Westerners to understand, and it tended to remain conceptual. So I taught the visualization practice of embodying and then feeding the demons I had developed during my month of feeding my own abandonment demon. And I taught students how to work this way with demons that were real issues in their lives, not just theoretical Buddhist concepts.

The demons I am referring to are not ghosts, goblins, or minions of Satan. When Machig was asked to define demons, she replied this way: "What we call demons are not materially existing individuals with huge black forms, frightening and terrifying anyone who sees them. A demon means anything which hinders liberation."

Our demons are not ancient gargoyles from eleventh-century Tibet. They are our present preoccupations, the issues in our lives blocking our experience of freedom. Our demons might come from the conflicts we have with our lover, anxiety we feel when we fly, or the discomfort we feel when we look at ourselves in the mirror. Fear of failure could be your particular demon, or addiction to tobacco, alcohol, drugs, pornography, or money. We might have a demon that makes us fear abandonment or a demon that causes us to hurt the ones we love. A person with an eating disorder might have a demon demanding huge amounts of sweet or fatty food. The demon of anorexia tells us that we have failed if we eat and that we will never be thin enough. A fear demon might be telling us we can't go up in high buildings or take a walk in the dark.

Although most people would say they don't believe in demons, the word is still commonly used, and when we hear it we know what it means. For example, someone might speak of her pattern of envy as her "jealousy demon," or we might use the expression "his demons came back to haunt him." It is common to speak of someone "wrestling with their demons," or to describe military veterans as "battling the demons of post-traumatic stress."

Demons are ultimately part of the mind and, as such, have no independent existence. Nonetheless, we engage with them as though they were real, and we believe in their existence — ask anyone who has fought post-traumatic stress, or addiction, or anxiety. Demons show up in our lives whether we provoke them or not, whether we want them or not. The mind perceives demons as real, so we get caught up in battling with them. Usually this habit of fighting against our perceived problems gives demons strength rather than weakening them. In the end, all demons are rooted in our tendency to create polarization. By understanding how to work with this tendency to try to dominate the perceived enemy and to see things as either/or, we free ourselves from demons by eliminating their very source.

We also tend to project our demons onto others. If we look at what we most despise in others, we usually see one of our own demons reflected back. If we look at those we criticize or try to control, we find the demons that we ourselves harbor. When we act as if we have no shadow, we are particularly vulnerable to being overwhelmed by our demons. Preachers and priests may have an especially hard time with this, because they are supposed to have overcome their demons, which only exacerbates the tendency to fight against them. This makes them susceptible to hypocrisy and self-destruction, like decrying the evils of sex while they are secretly engaged in the very kind of sex they publicly denounce.

The famous evangelical preacher Ted Haggard, minister of the largest evangelical church in Colorado Springs, preached against drug use, homosexuality, and gay marriage while he himself was secretly involved in homosexual encounters with a male prostitute in Denver. Married, with five children, Haggard gave the outward appearance of being a strictly heterosexual family man. After several years of regular visits from Haggard, the prostitute saw him on TV preaching against gay marriage. He was so disgusted by Haggard's hypocrisy that he went to the press and revealed that for three years Ted Haggard had been his client and had been buying drugs from him as well. After being forced to resign from the church he had founded, Haggard went into seclusion, still determined to "fight" his demons of forbidden desires.

The point here is that often we ridicule or criticize others who embody something we are trying to repress in ourselves. Certainly we all have urges we should not act on, such as violent impulses or the desire to steal or to abuse someone. However, repression is often not the most effective way to deal with unacceptable impulses. When we admit to them, by drawing them out of the closet and engaging with them consciously, they actually become less dangerous than when we fight them. Hidden away they only gain strength. The more we try to lock them up, the more devious and dangerous they become.

When we feed our demons using the five steps described in this book, we are integrating repressed and disowned parts of ourselves. When C. G. Jung was in personal crisis, he found that by personifying repressed parts of himself he could relieve his own internal pressure. After imagining and summoning up these embodied aspects of himself, he asked them questions, after which he found they often produced an image, and then the disturbance disappeared. Similarly, when you feed your demons you personify parts of yourself, interact with them, and integrate them through giving them what they need; in this way they can be liberated.

ARE DEMONS ALWAYS OBSTACLES?

It turns out that demons have a lot to offer us. For one thing, demons can act as a wake-up call. When we suffer from an outburst of anger, anxiety, or stress, instead of seeing it as something to suppress, fight against, or be ashamed of, we could see it as a demon demanding attention.

When Andrea, a thirty-eight-year-old teacher, came to volunteer at Tara Mandala, nothing seemed to go right for her. The firewood was wet, the chimney was blocked, her cabin was full of her unpacked belongings, and her mind was so cluttered she felt unable to meditate. She had recently broken up with her boyfriend of ten years. Suddenly she missed him terribly, and she began to wonder if breaking up with him had been a good idea.

She came to me and said she felt the world was conspiring against her. She longed to get things tidily arranged so she could really begin to meditate. Andrea thought her practice could truly begin when she was peacefully sitting on her cushion, meditating in her neatly arranged cabin. I encouraged her to see that the external situation was not the real demon, and that these upheavals were a wake-up call, a gift. She began to recognize these obstacles as her own hopes and fears, not outside forces undermining her. I suggested that her longing, her grief, and her frustration were not demonic obstacles to her spiritual practice, but invitations to apply what she was learning to what was *actually* happening, rather than to her idea of what *should* be happening. I led her through feeding the demons and taught her to work with feeding these demons on her own.

After she fed her demons, Andrea was able to shift the way she was viewing her situation. Rather than seeing events as conspiring against her, she saw these challenges as an invitation. In this way they were transformed into allies in her spiritual development. She was also able to recognize how much she was caught up in blaming the outside world for her inner state. We all tend to believe that our spiritual practice should be peaceful, but often the stickiest, most humiliating moments are the ones that generate the strongest experiences of awakening.

When my son, Cos, was twenty-five and entering a strict year-long retreat, his teacher, Adzom Rinpoche, said to him, "Remember, it's easy to practice meditation when the circumstances are good; the test of a good practitioner is to practice when the circumstances are difficult." This was very helpful to him when his demons came up during his retreat. It made him determined to work with the situation and feed his demons rather than just lament his condition or feel oppressed by his thoughts and emotions.

When difficulties come up in our lives, we can see them either as obstacles or as grist for the mill that has potential to bring us closer to awakening. Without these challenges and without recognizing our faults, we would spend our lives waiting for ideal circumstances instead of genuinely working on ourselves. In fact our "enemies," those who bring up the most in us, are our greatest teachers, and instead of seeing them as demons we could see them as gifts.

Fears, obsessions, and addictions are all parts of ourselves that have become "demonic" by being split off, disowned, and fought against. When we try to flee from our demons, they pursue us. By struggling with them as formless forces, we give them strength and may even succumb to them completely. For example, someone who fights alcoholism instead of feeding the root causes for the addiction may eventually die of liver disease. Someone who struggles with depression without coming to terms with its basis may eventually commit suicide. We need to recognize the futility of struggle, and feeling persecuted by outside circumstances is not the solution. We need to give our demons form and to give voice to those parts of ourselves that we feel persecuted by. Engaging with them, we can get at the source of the behaviors and transform that energy into an ally. This does not mean we indulge in destructive actions, but that we acknowledge our underlying needs. The practice of feeding demons makes this transformation possible.

Although throughout this book I am most frequently using the term "demon" to describe what we need to transform, think also about your gods, your obsessive longings. Consider that our hopes and desires can be as problematic as our fears. Fortunately, gods, like their demonic counterparts, can be turned into allies through the same five-step practice.

PART TWO

FEEDING YOUR DEMONS

4

HOW TO FEED YOUR DEMONS

The palate of hate departs,
Anger as soon as fed is dead;
'Tis starving makes it fat.

—*Emily Dickinson*

WHEN WE OBSESS about food issues, long for the perfect partner, or crave a cigarette, we give our demons strength, because we aren't really paying attention to the need beneath the desire. When we really pay attention and identify the deep call beneath the craving, we can learn to feed the real needs of the demon and not just indulge it or fight against it. Having been satisfied, it departs. Our demons get fatter if they are fought or ignored (which is also an active process), because they feed on the energy of our struggle against them. This is the principle behind fully attending to and nurturing rather than fighting or ignoring our demons.

If you feed your daughter a DVD when she really needs love, she's not going to be satisfied. If you ignore your daughter or fight against her, she will become more and more obnoxious until you truly give her your attention. But your impatient attention will not satisfy her. If we *pay attention* to a demanding child and give

51

her what she *needs*, not what she wants, she can relax and settle down. By stopping and discovering what she really needs, you are in a sense *paying* with your attention. The way to change things is to address the underlying issue, through feeding our demons what they actually need instead of what they seem to want. If we can get down to the fundamental need under the superficial desire, it usually involves love, compassion, and acceptance. We might want ice cream, for instance, but need a feeling of love. When we stop trying to dismiss demons by throwing them a bone, and instead *pay attention* and offer them our genuine presence, "the palate of hate departs."

When you drink another glass of wine instead of paying attention to your depression, it is not going to go away; in fact it will get stronger. Depression depletes you because it is "eating" at you unattended to while you are trying to get away from it. It's like having a leech sucking on you without your knowing it. But if you consciously pay attention to your demon of depression and feed it by following the five steps I will describe in this chapter, it will transform.

SETTING THE STAGE

Feeding a demon will take about half an hour. Choose a quiet place where you feel safe and comfortable. Arrange a time when you won't be interrupted. First thing in the morning, before you start your day, is a good time, but any time is fine if it is quiet. Set up two chairs or two cushions opposite each other: one for you and one for the demon and ally. Once you're set up you will want to keep your eyes closed until the end of the fifth step, so put the two seats (chairs or cushions) close enough to each other that you can feel the one in front of you with your eyes closed. Keeping your eyes closed will help you stay focused and present as you imagine this encounter with your demon. However, until you know the steps by heart, you'll need to glance at the abbreviated version of the five steps (in the appendix).

I suggest you keep a written record of your work. Ideally you'll keep a dedicated demon journal, but any notebook you use to keep track of the demons is fine (to read more about tracking your demons, see pages 77–79, on keeping a demon journal). If you have room, keep a set of cushions facing each other in a corner of your home, with your demon journal right there near the cushions, ready for your next meditation.

Nine Relaxation Breaths

At this point you are sitting in one of the chairs (or on one of the cushions), directly facing the other. You should now close your eyes.

Begin by taking nine deep abdominal breaths, which means breathing deeply until you can feel your abdomen expand. Place your hands on your stomach and notice it rise and fall. This guarantees you are breathing deeply, which will aid in relaxation.

As you inhale during the first three breaths, imagine your breath traveling to any *physical tension* you are holding in your body, and then imagine the exhalation carrying this tension away.

As you inhale with the next three breaths, imagine the breath traveling to any place in your body where you feel you are holding *emotional tension*, and then imagine the exhalation carrying this tension out of your body.

During the last three breaths, inhale into the part of your body where you are holding *mental tension* such as worries, thoughts about what you are doing, or fears that you can't be successful. Breathe into the place in your body where you are holding this mental tension and then release it with the exhalation.

Generating Your Motivation

After the nine relaxation breaths, once you feel settled and fully present, take a moment to relax and focus on your motive for undertaking this practice. I suggest you do it for the benefit of all beings, generating a deep, heartfelt wish to free yourself and all other life from suffering. This motive is important in shifting your focus from the ego's needs to compassion; it broadens the scope of your actions from mere selfish interest to the greater good.

Generating the right motivation before we do anything is very important. The great Tibetan teacher of the nineteenth century Patrul Rinpoche said:

> *What makes an action good or bad?*
> *Not how it looks, not whether it is big or small,*
> *But the good or evil motivation behind it.*

When we stop being caught up in our demons, we can help others and ourselves more effectively. Try to feel a positive motivation in your heart before proceeding with this practice, and a sense that you are doing this not just for yourself, but to benefit the larger world as well. This is known in Buddhism as establishing an altruistic intention, and it lends additional power to your practice.

THE FIVE STEPS OF FEEDING YOUR DEMONS

After the preliminaries you are ready to begin the five steps. In this section we will consider each step in depth. For a quick look at all five steps, see the abbreviated version in the appendix, page 257.

STEP 1: FIND THE DEMON

This first step has three phases:

- Deciding what demon you wish to work on
- Locating where you hold the demon in your body
- Observing the demon in your body

Deciding What Demon to Work On

A good way to choose what to focus on is to ask yourself the following questions:

- What is draining my energy?
- What is dragging me down?
- What is "eating" me?
- What incident has disturbed me recently?

It could be an old issue that keeps coming up, perhaps a persistent fear, addiction, pain, or illness. It could be a feeling about or reaction to another person, someone you are obsessed with, someone with whom you are in conflict, or someone who frightens you. (Rather than focusing on the actual person, you will be working on the feeling that comes up for you in relation to that person.) You might think about conflicts you've had with your lover or someone at work. It may be a demon of fear, clinging, or confusion. Our relationships are frequently the biggest triggers for our demons.

It is a good idea to choose the first thing that comes to mind when you think, "What demon do I want to work with?" Sometimes when something pops into your mind you'll think, "Oh no, not that. Anything but that." I recommend that you go ahead and choose that one.

You don't have to be afraid that this first demon is too big. In my experience, repressed demons (or "oh no" demons) are much more potent and destructive when we are avoiding them than when we become conscious of them. And when a big demon is fed, a lot of energy will be freed up to become your ally or protective energy.

Another good indication of a demon to meet is an emotion that keeps coming up. For example, you may find yourself subject to frequent and sudden bouts of rage, even though you do not think of yourself as an angry person. In that case you might choose to work with your anger demon. Other good possibilities might have to do with persistent issues in your life, such as depression, failed relationships, or money.

These are a few examples to help you get started. If nothing comes to mind, check in with your body. Do you have any chronic illnesses or other physical conditions? Do you have any pain or tension anywhere? If so, work with that; you will often find something under a physical sensation.

More likely, however, you will find yourself with such a long list of possible demons that you may have difficulty deciding which one to work with first. If this is the case, remember you can do this practice as many times and with as many demons as you like, so don't worry too much about picking the right one. Begin with whatever comes up most immediately.

In performing the practice of feeding your demon, you will probably discover demons that are related to or hidden under the first ones that show up. Demons can be like Russian dolls, nested one within the other. For example, you might begin with an addiction to coffee and discover below that a slave driver demon, and under that you might find a demon of fear of failure, and under that a demon telling you that you are stupid, and so on. Just start with whatever comes up first, and through your process of feeding your demons you will work through these layers; don't try to find the ultimate demon or work with more than one at once.

Locating the Demon in Your Body

Once you've determined what to work with, take a moment to tune in to your body. Grounding yourself in bodily sensation is a good way to bypass intellectualization; it helps to get you "out of your head," giving you direct access to your body's wisdom.

Often we spend so much time in our heads that we need to make an effort to get in touch with our bodies. Think about the

issue or demon you've decided to work with and let your awareness scan your body from head to toe, without any judgments,
simply being aware of the sensations that are present. Locate
where you are holding this energy by noticing where your attention goes in your body when you think about this issue. Once you
find the feeling, intensify it, exaggerate it.

You can also find where you hold the demon in your body by
consciously generating the emotion you're working with. For example, if you are working with anger, evoke the memory of a time
when anger came up strongly and then scan your body for sensations connected to this demon. Every emotion centers itself
somewhere in the body.

If your demon is the feeling of being pushed — of pressure to
achieve — this demon of stress may be something you live with
constantly, driving you from the moment that you wake up until
the moment that you go to bed. Where do you hold this tension
in your body? In your shoulders? Your neck? Remembering a situation when you felt particularly stressed might help locate this
energy in your body.

Observing the Demon in Your Body

Once you've found the demon's location in your body, you are
going to begin to explore it. This is an important step, because
one of the ways demons dominate us is by being amorphous, and
now you are beginning to make the demon conscious. Keeping
your eyes closed, let your imagination explore the physical sensation you've located. Here are some questions to ask yourself:

- What color is it?
- What shape does it have?
- Does it have a texture?
- What is its temperature?
- If it emitted a sound, what would it be?
- If it had a smell, what would it be?

STEP 2: PERSONIFY THE DEMON AND ASK IT WHAT IT NEEDS

In the second step you invite the demon to move from being simply a collection of sensations, colors, and textures that you've identified inside your body to becoming a living entity sitting right in front of you. Personifying the demon gives shape to what is often difficult to perceive and allows you to communicate with the demon. Encourage the sensation you have located in your body to appear before you personified in some way. It could be an animal, a person, a monster, or any other being that embodies the qualities you've identified. Don't try to control or decide what it will look like; let your unconscious mind produce the image. Personifying involves imagination, as you transform a sensation of feeling into a being. If something comes up that seems silly, like a cliché or a cartoon character, don't dismiss it or try to change it; work with whatever form shows up without editing it. However, it is helpful if the demon has a face, eyes, and appendages, because this will help you communicate with it. If the demon shows up as a tree or an inanimate object like a rock, ask it, "How would you look if you were an animate being?" Then see what appears, perhaps a gnarly tree becoming a bent-over old woman with swollen joints. Trust the image that appears.

Personifying the Demon

Here are some questions you might ask yourself to get a clearer sense of your demon:

- What size is it?
- Does it have arms and legs? If so, what are they like?
- What color is it?
- What is the surface of its body like?
- Does the demon have an age?
- Does it have a gender?
- What is its emotional state?
- How do I feel looking at it?

Make eye contact and notice the expression in its eyes. This is important in bringing it to life and making a felt connection.

Finally, look at the demon once more and see if you can notice something now that you didn't see before.

For example, pain I've been experiencing in my left shoulder is a stress demon that takes the form of a red, brittle, thin male. His feet are skeletal. His eyes are very intense and penetrating, and they look furious. He seems impatient with me. His hair is sticking up straight and is very rigid and fragile. He is cold even though he's red, and he's a little bigger than I am. He's middle-aged and intense. Precision in personifying the demon is important, because these images are communications from our unconscious mind. If you observe the demon closely, it will deliver far more information than something vague like "my fear demon." Your intellect may try to analyze the demon, or a series of different images may pop up, but stick to the first demon that appears. Don't second-guess yourself; it is usually best to go with the original image.

Asking the Demon What It Needs

The next part of this second step is to communicate directly with the demon, asking three questions, each of which brings you closer to understanding what will satisfy your demon. This is your opportunity to directly engage with the demon, and as soon as you ask the questions you will change places with the demon. The three questions should be spoken aloud in the order they are listed, because they gradually move you toward the kind of nectar you will be feeding the demon:

> *What do you want from me?*
> *What do you need from me?*
> *How will you feel if you get what you need?*

Then, as I said, once you have asked these questions, don't wait for an answer; change places with the demon. You need to become the demon to know the answers.

STEP 3: BECOME THE DEMON

With your eyes still closed, move to the seat you have set up in front of you, facing your original seat, and imagine yourself as the demon. Take a deep breath or two, and feel yourself becoming this demon. Vividly recall the being that was personified in front of you, and imagine you are "in the demon's shoes." Take a moment to adjust to your new identity before answering the three questions, imagining your ordinary self in front of you.

Often we think we know what the demon must be feeling when we look at it, but when we become the demon, we feel very different. A demon that seemed threatening actually could be afraid and just acting that way to protect itself. This step can be one of the most surprising parts of the process, so make the effort to change places, even if it seems silly or awkward. Then answer the three questions aloud, in the first person, from the demon's point of view, like this:

What I want from you is . . .
What I need from you is . . .
When my need is met, I will feel . . .

The red, spiky stress demon I mentioned above might answer the first question this way: "I want you to hurry up and get more done so you will be more successful."

It's very important that these questions make the distinction between wants and needs, because many demons will want your life force, or everything good in your life, or to control you, but that's not what they *need*. Often what they need is hidden beneath what they say they want, which is why we ask the second question, probing a little deeper. The demon of alcoholism might *want* alcohol but need something quite different, like safety or relaxation. Until we get to the need underlying the craving, the craving will continue.

In response to the question "What do you need?" the stress demon might respond: "What I actually need is to feel secure."

Having learned that beneath the stress demon's desire to hurry and do more lies a need to feel secure, you still must find out how the demon will feel if it gets what it needs. *This will tell you what to feed the demon.* Thus, having been asked, "How will you feel if you get what you need?" the stress demon might answer: "I will feel like I can let go and finally relax." Now you know to feed this demon relaxation.

With a disease like cancer the demon might say, "I want your life force, all of it." And responding to "What do you need?" the demon might say, "I need strength." And if to the question "How will you feel if you get what you need?"—in this case, strength—the demon replies, "I'll feel powerful," then you know to feed the demon power. Be sure the answer to the third question is a feeling. For example, the cancer demon might have said, "I will feel huge." But hugeness is not a feeling; you need to know how it will *feel* when it gets what it needs. The *feeling* behind hugeness might be one of power, as it is here.

We might think feeding power to a demon like cancer will only make it grow, but the paradox is that by directly addressing the demon's underlying need, we diminish its strength. This is the opposite of some alternative approaches to cancer in which you visualize the cancer being attacked and destroyed by armies of white cells. The idea is that if the demon's need is addressed and satisfied through the nectar, then the cancer in the body decreases.

The addiction to cigarettes might *want* a cigarette and *need* security, and if it gets security it will *feel* peaceful. So the nectar will be a feeling of peace. By feeding the demon the emotional feeling that underlies the desire for the substance, we address the core issue instead of just the symptoms. And if the stress demon that wants success ultimately needs to feel relaxed, feeding it a feeling of relaxation will put an end to its compulsive activity.

STEP 4: FEED THE DEMON AND MEET THE ALLY

This step has two phases: feeding the demon and meeting the ally. If you feel complete after feeding the demon to full satisfaction, you can, if you wish, move directly from feeding the demon to the fifth step. It's not necessary to meet the ally in order to get the benefit from the five-step practice. However, meeting the ally can be a richly rewarding part of the process.

Feeding the Demon

Now we've reached the crucial moment when we actually feed the demon. Return to your original position and face the demon. Take a moment to settle back into your own body before you envision the demon in front of you again.

First separate your awareness from your body so that you feel as if your consciousness is outside it and your awareness is just an observer of this process. Then begin to imagine your body melting into a nectar that consists of whatever the demon has told you it ultimately will feel if it gets what it needs. As your imagination gives form to the nectar, let go of your attachment to your body and imagine your consciousness leaving it. In the traditional practice of Chöd your consciousness leaves through the top of your head and joins up with a visualized form of the fierce wisdom mother Troma, a blue-black dancing goddess who oversees the transformation of the body into nectar. You may imagine this, or you may simply bring your awareness to bear on the experience of your body as it becomes nectar. In either case allow your body to dissolve. You may find yourself dissolving feet first, gradually ending with your head. You might dissolve at both ends and toward your heart. Or you might dissolve all in one moment, spontaneously.

The nectar is usually liquid, but it might also be a gaseous substance, or whatever arises from your imagination. Some people envision their nectar as steam or smoke, while others may imagine something like cream — or even ice cream! Note its color as well as the method of its delivery. Does it come in a container that the demon will drink from or bathe in, or is it just a river or stream of liquid that flows toward the demon? This nectar is a distillation of whatever the demon describes in answer to the third question, that is, the *feeling* it will have when it gets what it needs. For example, the demon might have said it will feel powerful, or loved, or accepted when it gets what it needs. So the essence or quality of the nectar should be just that: power, love, or acceptance.

Give free rein to your imagination in seeing how the nectar will be absorbed by the demon. See the demon drinking in your offering of nectar through its mouth or through the pores of its skin, or inhaling it, or taking it in some other way. Whatever you imagine, try to see it clearly and in detail. Continue visualizing the nectar flowing into the demon and imagine that there is an infinite supply of this nectar and that you are offering it with a feeling of limitless generosity. As you feed your demon, watch it carefully, as it is likely to begin to change. Does it look different in any way? Does it morph into a new being altogether?

What happens when the demon is completely satisfied? At the moment of total satiation, its appearance usually changes significantly. It may become something completely new or disappear into smoke or mist. There's nothing it's "supposed" to do, so just observe what happens; let the process unfold without trying to create a certain outcome. Whatever develops will arise spontaneously when the demon is fed to its total satisfaction. It is very important that the demon be fed to *complete* satisfaction. Your offering should not be partial or conditional. If your demon seems insatiable, imagine how it would appear if it were completely satisfied.

Once I went through the five steps with a woman from Los Angeles who had a history of being physically and verbally abused. She had internalized this as a demon of self-loathing. When I talked to her about the fourth step, she said, "Look, I don't believe this is going to work for me. I have a hateful voice inside me that never leaves me alone, not even for a minute." She was in tears, feeling hopeless.

When she got to the fourth step with her eyes closed, suddenly she started laughing. When the practice was over and we were discussing it, she said, "I don't believe it. After I fed him, my inner-hater demon turned around and walked out of the room, closing the door behind him. When I looked at the door there was a sign hanging on it that said 'Gone Fishing.' " She couldn't stop laughing, and for the first time in years she felt free of her demon of self-loathing.

Meeting the Ally

You may remember from the story of Machig and the water spirits in chapter one that once Machig had offered herself as food to the attacking nagas, they transformed into allies and pledged to protect her and her followers. The same holds true for us: when we offer ourselves as nectar to the demon, its negative energy becomes transformed into a positive force. Now, as the demon resolves through satiation, we have an opportunity to meet that force in personified form, and to see exactly how this transformed energy could become a positive and protective presence in our lives.

A satisfied demon may turn into a benevolent figure, which may be the ally. This ally could be an animal, a bird, a human, a mythic god or bodhisattva, a child, or a familiar person. If there is a figure present after the demon is satiated completely, ask it if it is the ally. If it is not, you can leave that being there and invite an ally to appear beside it. The demon may have turned into smoke, melted into a puddle, or simply disintegrated. If the demon has disappeared and there is no figure present, you can still meet the ally by inviting an ally to appear in front of you. Whatever form the ally takes, notice the details of its appearance. Try to see the look in its eyes, its size, its color, and what it is wearing. If it is an inanimate object or a plant, invite it to become a personified being.

Again speaking aloud, ask the ally one or all of the following questions:

How will you help me?
How will you protect me?
What pledge or commitment do you make to me?
How can I gain access to you?

Then change places immediately and become the ally, just as you did in step three, when you became the demon. Having become the ally, take a moment to fully inhabit this body. Notice how it feels to be this protective guardian. Then, speaking as the ally, answer the questions above. Try to be as specific as possible.

I will help you by . . .
I will protect you by . . .
I pledge I will . . .
You can gain access to me by . . .

Once the ally has articulated how it will serve and protect you, and how you can summon it, return to your original place. Take a moment to settle back into yourself and see the ally in front of you. Then imagine you are receiving the help and the commitment the ally has pledged. Feel this supportive energy enter you and take effect. Allow yourself to bask awhile in the stream of positive energy coming from the ally.

Finally, imagine the ally itself melting into you, and feel its deeply nurturing essence integrating with you. Notice how you feel when the ally has dissolved into you. Realize the ally is actually an inseparable part of you, and then allow yourself to dissolve into emptiness, which naturally takes you to the fifth and final step.

The more intense and formidable the demon was, the greater the power of the ally, for it is the intensity of the demon that becomes the power source of the ally. To transfer the power of the ally to our daily lives, we need to call on the ally. Sometimes just keeping the image or words of the ally in mind is enough. You can also keep a representation of it in a place where you will see it frequently.

If the figure that initially remained at the end of feeding the demon was not the ally, that figure will still be present alongside the ally. So after you have questioned the ally and received its energy, integrate both the ally and the other figure into you and go on to the fifth step. I once saw a young child at the end of the fourth step, but this little girl told me she was not the ally. Moments later, a tall figure like a black Madonna appeared next to her: this was the ally. So while I dialogued with the Madonna-like figure, the young child waited. Then I dissolved them both into me and entered the fifth step.

An example of the power of the ally comes from Frances, a fifty-three-year-old psychotherapist and doctor. She was working with a feeling in her breast that had been frightening her for quite a long time. It felt as if a funnel in her breast was draining her life energy. The demon she saw when she took the second step was very big and black, a wolflike creature standing on his hind feet. He had a huge snout, sharp teeth, and red eyes, which were fixated on her. His fur crackled with electricity and every so often gave off a shower of white sparks, and he had long, razorlike claws.

When Frances identified with the demon she felt huge and mighty, whereas her normal self seemed very small. The demon wanted her normal self to serve him, to do only what he wanted her to do. By achieving this, the demon said, it would feel powerful: big and strong.

Frances melted her body into a nectar of power and strength and offered this to the wolfish demon. He drank and drank, and as he did so his fur got lighter and lighter in color, until it was almost white. His eyes became blue. Finally he looked like a huge husky, gazing faithfully at her. He said he was her ally.

When she asked the ally how he would serve her, he answered that he wanted to give her his wisdom, which she could access by looking into his eyes. Frances was deeply touched by his obvious devotion to her as he lay down, placing his head on her knee.

After resting in the open space at the end of the five steps, Frances found that the funnel-like feeling in her breast had disappeared. The blue-eyed husky-ally accompanied her everywhere from that day on, and when she went back to work she felt protected. The huge, white husky still accompanies her today. When she feels lonely or insecure, he lies at her side. And when she looks into his blue eyes, it is as if she is looking into the sky, only they are reflecting back wisdom.

The ally can serve a supportive role long after the session in which you fed your demon has ended. Learn to use the ally, perhaps by drawing it and keeping its image posted in a place where you see it frequently. Also be sure to ask how to access the ally. One woman who needed to be more grounded was told by her ally to evoke it by touching the wooden beads that she always wore on her wrist. Some people purchase a stuffed animal or a statue to remind them of their ally. Such reminders of your inner resources can be very helpful.

After meeting the ally, you can choose to access the ally in a separate session dedicated to creating a dialogue with the ally. After taking the nine relaxation breaths, invite the ally to appear. Then you can ask it a question. Change places, answer, come back to your original seat, and ask another question, until you're satisfied. This allows you to enter a deeper relationship with your ally.

STEP 5: REST IN AWARENESS

When you have finished feeding the demon to complete satisfaction and the ally has been integrated, you and the ally dissolve into emptiness. Then you just rest in the awareness that is present. When the mind takes a break for even a few seconds, a kind of relaxed awareness replaces the usual stream of thoughts. We need to allow this and not fill this space with anything else; just let it be. There is no "me," and no "demon"; here we have transcended the self and its fixations. You may experience this as relaxation or peacefulness, but don't try to force this or to name it. Just let yourself be at ease. You can extend this meditative state for as long as you wish, maybe returning a couple of times to the sensation and immediate awareness that first arose as you dissolved into emptiness. But don't become heavy-handed about it; just rest in a relaxed state, and finish when your mind moves to something else. Although in a sense there's "nothing happening," in fact this fifth step is the most important moment in the process of feeding your demons.

There are two principal benefits that flow from the practice of feeding your demons. One is transforming our demons into allies so we can move from being dominated by internal and external struggle to accessing the energy tied up in the conflict. The other is a subtler but even more important fruit of the practice. This is the opening that emerges in the fifth step, a window into a state that is free from subconscious chatter, emotional distractions, and the many fixations that make up our daily lives. It is not unlike what happens after you've done hard physical labor and you flop on the ground exhausted, only this is a mental flop rather than a physical one.

Some people describe it as peace, others as relaxation, and yet others as a great vastness. I like calling it "the gap," or the space between thoughts. Usually when we experience the gap we have a tendency to want to fill it up immediately, much the way we come home to an empty house and tend to turn on the TV, make a phone call, or get on the Internet. We are uncomfortable with empty space. In the fifth step, rather than filling this space, you rest in it. Even if this open awareness only occurs for a moment, it's the beginning of knowing our true nature. As you become comfortable with this nonreferential state, you begin to move away from habitual clinging. We are typically so caught up in our difficulties and thoughts that we don't experience this state, so resting in it is like letting ourselves float in the ocean and be rocked by it instead of giving in to our fears of drowning and struggling against it.

In this chapter we have seen how to perform the five steps through which you feed your demon, find your ally, and rest in awareness. When using the five steps, try not to leave anything out. Each step makes its own important contribution to the process, from the relaxation breaths at the beginning to the meditation at the end. Following the five steps carefully will bring you much better results than if you skip over some parts. For instance, by assuming that you know what the demon needs instead of actually changing places with it and experiencing the demon's point of view, you lose the experience of becoming the demon.

Now let's take a look at an example of a five-step practice, along with some additional guidelines and suggestions.

5

THE FIVE STEPS IN ACTION

One does not become enlightened by imagining figures of
light but by making the darkness conscious.

—*Carl G. Jung*

THE PREVIOUS CHAPTER explained how to perform the five
steps. This chapter begins with an example of someone going
through the five-step practice and then will look at several ways
you can develop the practice to make it even more effective.

KATE'S STORY

Kate had very critical parents, who indirectly were always telling
her she was not worthy of love. Not surprisingly she began to
hate herself. Although she grew up and married, eventually her
husband left her. Kate couldn't keep a job. She felt deeply unworthy of love and acted self-destructively.

Her inner voice constantly told her she was not good enough,
that she was a loser, and that she should just give up on life. This
was her self-hate demon, which was running rampant. Although
she remained unaware of how much it influenced her, it disrupted
everything. The voice did, however, provide a kind of negative

security, familiar but toxic. Here, in brief, is how Kate dealt with her self-hate demon.

Step 1: Find the Demon

After doing the nine relaxation breaths and generating an altruistic intention for her practice, Kate closes her eyes and sinks into awareness of her body, trying to locate the feeling of worthlessness and self-loathing. She remembers an intense attack of negativity that triggered her self-loathing. After being fired from a promising job, she had called her mother hoping for sympathy, but instead of offering support, Kate's mother blamed her for losing the job. Filled with anger and self-hatred, Kate cut her arms for the first time. Recalling this event, she suddenly feels an intense sensation in her heart. She experiences it as cold, blue-purple, and lacerating, like a shard of shattered glass. It's piercing and painful. Her heart aches.

Step 2: Personify the Demon and Ask It What It Needs

Kate now imagines the embodiment of this feeling. It takes the form of a tall, thin male figure. He's ice-blue and his bony arms end in claws. He's looking at her with disdain. His teeth are pointed and yellow, and his mouth opens as if he's going to bite her. His eyes are small and fierce. When she takes a second look, she notes that the surface of his body is covered with fine, spiky blue thorns.

Kate asks him aloud:

"What do you want from me?

75

"What do you need from me?

"How will you feel if you get what you need?"

Step 3: Become the Demon

Before he answers, she changes places and becomes him, occupying the chair opposite her own, and takes a moment to become the demon, to live in his skin. She pauses to experience what he is feeling before answering the questions. Inhabiting his body, she realizes that he's incredibly bitter and feels threatened and battered himself. To the question "What do you want?" he replies, "I want you to suffer, because you are so worthless and stupid."

To the question "What do you need?" he answers, "I need you to be with me, and to stop trying to escape from me. I need you to accept me and love me."

To the question "How will you feel if you get what you need?" he answers: "I'll be able to relax. I'll feel love."

Step 4: Feed the Demon and Meet the Ally

Returning to her original seat, Kate sees the self-hate demon in front of her. She now knows she needs to feed him love. She imagines her body melting into an infinite ocean of loving nectar, and then imagines that the demon takes this nectar in through every pore of his icy blue body all at once.

As he absorbs the nectar, the demon's appearance changes. His body softens and his color fades. After a while he turns into a gray horse with soft nostrils and gentle, dark eyes.

Kate asks the gray horse if it is the ally. When it nods its noble head, she asks how it will help her in the future, how it will protect her, and what pledge it will make to her. She then changes places with the ally and becomes the gray horse. She hears herself reply, "I will carry you to places you haven't been before, where you can't go alone. I will lend you my strength to do things in the world. When things are difficult, come see me and rest your head on my neck. I will protect you by giving you strength in yourself."

Kate returns to her seat and, gazing at the horse in front of her, receives its strength and takes in its pledge. As these flow into her, she feels joy rising inside her heart. Eventually the horse itself dissolves into her completely and she feels a vast surge of strength within herself. Then she and the ally both dissolve into emptiness.

Step 5: Rest in Awareness

At this point Kate feels peace. She rests, allowing herself to relax in that state of open awareness. She doesn't need to "practice" the fifth step; it is just there. This is not a state that she thinks herself into; it is the natural spaciousness that comes with the dissolution of the demon and the integration of the ally.

KEEPING A DEMON JOURNAL

In the previous chapter I recommended that you create a written record of your experience of the five steps in as much detail as possible. As you are writing, insights or associations may bubble up, so be sure to jot those down too. If you are working with a particular demon over time, track your progress in this journal. Also make a note of any effects you've experienced as a result of the demon feeding. You may notice changes in your health, behavior, or emotional state to which you should pay particular attention. Writing about feeding your demons can help stabilize and reinforce the process as it unfolds.

If you like, draw an image of the demon and of the ally, in addition to writing about your experience. Don't think you have to be trained in art to do this—it is just for you to use for your own demon work. Some people buy a big unlined journal and draw pictures of their demons and allies with felt-tipped pens, oil crayons, or colored pencils. (For further explorations of using art with feeding your demons, see chapter seven.) You decide what kind of record you would like to keep, whether it's a fully illustrated, detailed account, or just simple notes. But do your best to record the five steps in as much detail as you can, along with whatever thoughts, associations, or memories are triggered by the demon.

Here are some questions you might ask yourself as you write:

- What demon did I work with?
- Where was it held in my body and what color, texture, and temperature did it have?
- What did my demon look like?
- What was the look in my demon's eyes?
- What was it like to become my demon? Was it different from what I expected by looking at it?
- What did my demon want?
- What did my demon need?
- What feeling was it looking for in getting what it needed?

- What did I feed my demon?
- How did its appearance change as I fed it?
- What remained when it was completely satisfied?
- What did my ally look like?
- What did it pledge to me?
- How will it protect me?
- How did I feel when the ally dissolved into me?
- What was the resting phase like, in the fifth step?
- How can I apply this experience to my everyday life?
- What changes do I want to make as a result of feeding this demon?
- What can I do to be able to access my ally?

Writing itself can trigger a chain reaction of further insights. For example, while writing down her experiences with a demon of insecurity about her appearance, Clarissa, a forty-year-old physical therapist, remembered that her mother, who had been poor as a child, had always been embarrassed about her own clothes. No wonder she was constantly critical of Clarissa's appearance! The memory of an old photo of her mother as an awkwardly dressed child of five flashed into Clarissa's mind as she wrote. She began to see connections between her mother's demons and her own. She had always had difficulty getting along with her mother, but through the process of writing about the demon, Clarissa's compassion for her mother increased, which opened up space for the two of them to grow much closer. Had she not taken the time to write about her process, this insight might not have had a chance to make itself known.

DEALING WITH RESISTANCE

While feeding our demons we can run into various forms of resistance. When we're working with long-standing issues or physical conditions, it can be difficult to let go of the problem and let the demon reach complete satisfaction. Our problems can become so much a part of our identity that unconsciously—and sometimes even consciously—we may cling to them. On some level we may be asking ourselves, "Who would I be without my problem?" Though we might not want to admit it, we become attached to our "stuff," our issues. They become a kind of full-time job. Since so much of our energy may be tied up in being a victim, an addict, or an angry, self-righteous person, we become afraid of the space that could open up if our problem dissolved. Unconsciously we may cling to our demons and may not allow them to become fully satisfied in the fourth step. In more serious cases we may become emotionally addicted to the energy of the demon. Someone with a rage demon, for example, might take perverse pleasure in exploding at people or intimidating them.

The most effective way to work with this resistance is to imagine how the demon *would* look if it *were* completely satisfied after you fed it in the fourth step. I usually recommend this "as if" approach to resistance because it effectively bypasses the tendency to hold on to the needy demon. I have found that imagining in detail how the demon would look if it was completely satisfied gives you full access to the freedom of the fifth step, even though we have, in a sense, tricked the demon.

Another kind of resistance that may come up is resentment toward the demon, which makes it difficult for you to be generous. If this happens, remind yourself that fighting this demon hasn't worked, so it might be worthwhile to try another approach. Then see if you can feed the demon even just a little bit. This creates an opening for gradually releasing the resentment and feeding the demon to its complete satisfaction.

If you meet with resistance in the form of difficulty getting answers from the demon about what it wants or needs, try asking, "Why are you hanging around, what are you trying to get?" If you can't see the embodiment of the demon clearly, go back to the physical sensation in step one and wait to get that really clear before trying to see the demon.

If you are experiencing resistance, check to be sure you are faithfully following the five steps. If not, please try again, and follow the instructions closely. These steps are carefully organized and worded to make your process successful.

ASKING FOR ASSISTANCE

It's not uncommon for a lot of emotions to come up as you begin the five steps. You may find yourself weeping or upset. Still, I encourage you to move ahead with the process unless you truly feel you don't want to. Rest assured that it is completely normal to experience powerful emotions when you finally face things you have been avoiding. By continuing the five-step practice in spite of these emotions, you will most likely end up feeling relieved and released. Sometimes, as we have seen, we have to overcome our anger with our demon to feed it compassion, or overcome our fears in order to feed it love. But if we can allow ourselves to try to feed the demon, something always shifts.

If you start to feel overwhelmed when facing a big demon, ask yourself, "Who might help give me the strength to make the offering? Whose assistance do I want?" Then imagine inviting a wise being, a dear friend, or a spiritual teacher to witness the process and to provide assistance and moral support.

You may already have a spiritual guide to turn to in times of need, or a friend, therapist, or teacher you trust. If so, imagine that he or she is in the space above the demon in front of you, helping you let go of your fear or anger so you can feed this demon. This supportive being acts as your compassionate helper as you feed the demon.

FEEDING YOUR DEMONS WITH A PARTNER

Feeding your demons with a partner can be effective when you feel you could use some support during the practice. When working with a partner, one person takes the active role while the other acts as a witness, and then you change places.

The Setup

As you begin, set up three cushions or chairs, one for the witness and the other two for the active partner and the demon. The seats for the demon and the active partner should face each other. The witness sits perpendicular to the active partner and the demon, back far enough to see both positions easily but close enough for it to feel intimate.

Confidentiality

Before beginning to feed your demons with a partner, it is essential to agree on guidelines for confidentiality. You should establish that whatever takes place in the joint session will not be discussed with anyone else unless specific permission has been granted. Then make sure that you live up to this commitment, without any wiggle room, without even making a joke. Don't even allow the session to come up in conversation between the two of you unless the active partner wants to talk about it. Seal the practice with confidentiality and respect this boundary completely.

The Witness

The witness should be supportive and not judgmental in any way. The role of the witness is to serve as an empathetic presence to facilitate the process. The witness is not there to act as a therapist, or to consult with or shape their partner's experience, but simply to hold the space for the work, and keep the partner on track with the five steps. The witness should have a copy of the five steps (refer to the short version in the appendix if necessary).

When the practice is under way, the witness should listen closely and pay careful attention to every nuance of the active partner's expression and body language in order to stay fully attuned to what that partner is experiencing. For example, a subtle smile might appear when the demon is fully satisfied, signaling the need for a quiet time when the active partner can sit in peace.

If you are serving as witness and your partner starts to weep during the process, I recommend you continue with the five steps. I have often seen tears or fear at the beginning of the practice, but by the end the tears are gone and something important has shifted. However, if your partner seems extremely distressed, you might ask if they'd like to come back to meet the demon at another time. The witness should never suggest that his or her partner hasn't gone deep enough, or hasn't picked the right demon, or critique the process in any way.

The witness can serve another valuable function by acting as a scribe, recording what happens in the five steps, but if this is too much, simply guide your partner verbally. A less experienced witness can act as a guide using the five steps, keeping a written copy of the short version in the appendix at hand to refer to. But it's best if the witness has the steps memorized and can guide his or her partner without hesitation. It is also important that the practice not degenerate into a conversation between the active partner and the witness, instead of between the active partner and the demon.

The Practice

Before beginning, the witness might ask, "Do you know what demon you want to work with?" The active partner will then describe the issue or demon he or she wants to work with. If she is not sure, it's fine to talk a little bit about what demon or god she might want to feed, until a decision is reached.

The witness guides her partner in the nine relaxation breaths. Then the witness suggests performing the meditation for the benefit of all beings, and the witness and partner generate an altruistic motivation together. The active partner keeps her eyes closed while the witness keeps hers open and on her partner. As the active partner begins, she reports to the witness what she is seeing during the practice.

Assuming the active partner doesn't know the practice by heart, the witness guides her through the steps. When the active partner gets to the fourth step of actually feeding the demon, the witness can periodically ask, "What's happening now? Has it changed?"

The witness can ask after a while, "Is it completely satisfied?" If the demon is resisting and not becoming satisfied, the witness might suggest that the active partner imagine how the demon (or god) would look if it was completely satisfied. Then the witness can ask the active partner to nod his or her head when the demon appears to be fully satisfied.

When the demon is satisfied, or looks as if it is, the witness asks if the active partner would like to meet the ally and proceed with step four. Remember, the active partner has been doing all the talking to the demon or ally, not the witness. Continue through the rest of step four, with the active partner describing what she is experiencing with the ally, until she and her ally have dissolved into emptiness. At this point both the witness and her partner enter meditation and are silent (step five). When the process feels complete to the active partner, the partners change places so that the active partner becomes the witness. It's best not to have any discussion between turns; you can talk later, after both of you are finished, if you wish.

Remember, during the five steps the active partner is always speaking in the first person. If she is speaking as the demon, for example, she would say, "I need you to stop running around and start listening to me." This is far more effective and immediate than reporting to the witness, "The demon says it needs me to stop running around and pay attention."

It's also a good idea to arrange a regular time to meet your partner to feed your gods or demons. This keeps the practice going without the need to compare calendars and negotiate a new time every week, which makes it easier for both parties.

DOING THE FIVE STEPS WITH A THERAPIST

If you're interested in using this practice with a psychotherapist, try to find a licensed therapist or counselor who has experience working with imagery. Gestalt therapists and Jungian analysts both meet this requirement, as do practitioners of other kinds of psychotherapy that personify parts of the psyche. If you show your therapist the five steps and explain the principles behind feeding your demons, he or she may be willing to act as your witness.

In the case of counselors who work with addiction or eating disorders, the demon is obvious, and each session will focus on that demon. However, in every session the therapist should begin at the beginning and guide the client through steps one and two; no one should assume the demon will manifest the same way each time. Even when it's a familiar issue, steps one and two should be approached fresh every session. The therapist acts as witness in the manner described above, but the therapist may also discuss the experience afterward with the client, in the context of the ongoing therapeutic relationship.

USING THE FIVE STEPS TOGETHER WITH OTHER MEDITATION PRACTICES

The practice of feeding demons has been combined successfully with several kinds of meditation practice. Teachers and ministers from various traditions have found the five steps of feeding the demons helpful when someone they are trying to guide is stuck or experiencing a profound upheaval of some kind. If you work with a meditation teacher or a pastor and he or she is willing, he/she can function as a witness much the way a therapist would.

If you are meditating on your own, without a teacher, you can begin a meditation session with the five steps and just extend the fifth step into your meditation practice. For example, some meditation teachers suggest that their students practice feeding their demons at the beginning of their meditation and then shift into their normal meditation after the fifth step. This can be particularly useful when you wish to meditate but something is preventing you from concentrating. Feeding a demon can relieve the blockage, freeing up the meditation practice to continue. A student may also perform the five steps separately, without connecting them to their meditation practice.

MAINTENANCE

My motto is "A demon a day keeps the doctor away." But really it's up to you how often you feed your demons. If you are working with an acute situation, such as an addictive behavior or an emotional crisis, I suggest that you feed your demons at least once a day, and if possible several times a day. You may also discover layers of demons that require separate sessions. For example, I might begin with a pain in my shoulder and then discover I have a workaholic demon and below that a fear demon of not being good enough. Learning how to feed your demons is a practice, and like any worthwhile practice it needs to be performed repeatedly. If your need is not urgent, you can always feed your demons "as needed." However, practicing only at times of crisis is not as effective as doing it regularly.

It is possible to transform even the most ingrained demons. Sometimes a demon can be reactivated after a long time if triggering circumstances arise, but sometimes we can succeed in freeing ourselves permanently. If you have a deep-seated demon, it is a good idea to periodically check in with it by thinking of it and scanning your body for any sensations or "demon deposits." If you find something, feed the demon again using the five-step practice.

If you want to really develop the practice, I suggest feeding your demons at least one hundred times and keeping a journal. Cultivate some demon-feeding partners with whom you meet regularly. Allow the fifth step to gradually lengthen and become a doorway into meditation. Don't skip any part of the process, thinking you already know it. If you have no better option, you can practice the five steps while lying in bed, sitting on a park bench, or wherever you may find yourself. This is not ideal, but it's far better than not practicing at all.

In these atypical feedings, if it is too awkward to physically change places, you can become the demon or the ally without this step. I have led people through the process this way during lectures, and I have done it myself this way at night while lying awake. However, whenever possible, I recommend going through the full process: it makes such a difference. There is no substitute for actually sitting in the demon's seat and looking out at the world from inside its skin.

6

HYDRAS: DEMON COMPLEXES

Making use of unfavorable conditions
Was taught by venerable Machig.
To consider adversity as a friend
Is the instruction of Chöd.

—Machig Labdrön

I CALL a demon complex a hydra because it is a many-headed tangle of interrelated gods and demons. Remember the story of Hercules battling the Hydra, a vicious water spirit, from chapter one? It had many legs and nine heads, one of which was immortal. When Hercules cut off one head, two more appeared in its place. Working with a hydra will gradually lead us to the core issues of the complex, but until we get at that immortal head and feed it, the complex can always generate new limbs and heads. One characteristic of working with a hydra is surprise when you discover interconnected demons you had never considered before.

Melissa had an experience like this when she started working with her anxiety around food. A businesswoman in her fifties, Melissa runs a mail-order business, has ten employees, and is very successful. She is also overweight and has developed health problems related to obesity. She has struggled with anxiety and food issues for most of her life, overeating in an attempt to find comfort. Food is her way of managing her emotions. When she overeats she hardly tastes her food.

Before she learned how to feed her demons, Melissa found it difficult to take pleasure in being with people. She was gradually isolating herself. As she got fatter, she felt shame about her body and isolated herself even more. When she ate pasta, she had one plate after another. She also ate ice cream a quart at a time.

Earlier in her life Melissa had had trouble with nicotine and alcohol, and it was when she gave them up that she began overeating. She used to drink by herself, and then she started to eat by herself instead. She often has the feeling she's made a mistake and apologizes when it isn't necessary. She has always longed for "mother love," and has never known why this longing was so loaded with grief. She has a complex constellation of intertwined demons, a hydra.

The first time Melissa tried to feed her food-anxiety demon, when she personified it in step two, it disappeared before she could ask it the three questions and really work with it. By returning to the sensation in her body and focusing on it, she was able to bring the demon back. She felt such waves of emotion that she found it difficult to stay focused; she kept "spacing out." The demon was a large gray octopus-like being with sad drunken eyes. When she was finally able to ask the three questions and then trade places with the demon, Melissa was surprised by the answers the demon gave her.

"What I want," the demon said, "is sex." Melissa had not expected the demon to say that; she didn't realize her food anxiety had anything to do with sex. This was an "Aha!" moment for her, as pieces of a puzzle fell together.

Melissa realized there was a connection between sexual abuse she had experienced as a child and her addiction to food. She had been molested by an uncle when she was young, and when this was discovered by Melissa's mother, she reacted in a way that caused Melissa to feel deep shame. Then Melissa acted out sex games with her little brother, which her mother discovered. Again she shamed Melissa, and this time she also withdrew her affection. Melissa was just reenacting what had happened to her, a natural response, but now she had the double trauma of sexual abuse from her uncle and the loss of her mother's nurturing. This was the immortal head at the core of her hydra complex, the source of her anxiety and the legs of the hydra: addiction, shame, guilt, insecurity, and longing for her mother's love.

"What I need," the demon continued, "is affection and love. If I got what I needed, I would feel fully nurtured, cared for, wanted, and loved, just the way a baby is." This felt important to Melissa, because she realized that this was the way she had felt before the sexual abuse began. Melissa wrote in her journal that this feeling was like being "whole and content with no fear."

When Melissa fed the demon, it became a happy baby, but this turned out not to be the ally. After some prompting from her demon work partner, Melissa was able to invite an ally to appear. The ally, a wise motherly figure with long black hair, pledged to keep Melissa safe and to always be there when Melissa needed her. Over time Melissa has continued feeding the various parts of her hydra and working with her core issues of shame and longing for affection. Since feeding her hydra, she has stopped overeating and lost weight. She still cooks delicious food, but now she eats one plate and feels satisfied. She is rapidly gaining confidence, and no longer doubts herself all the time, and she is developing friendships and a connection to a Buddhist community.

Melissa's work with the anxiety demon brought her to the realization that the sexual abuse she had suffered earlier in her life, and her mother's reaction to it, was at the root of her constellation of problems, the core of her many-headed hydra.

Peggy also had a hydra demon, which she only recently discovered. More than thirty years earlier, when she was a teenager, Peggy had been in a relationship and found out she was pregnant. During her eighth month of pregnancy, she discovered that her boyfriend was in a love relationship with another woman in a distant city.

When the other woman learned about Peggy and the pregnancy, she did not end the relationship with the man with whom they both were involved, but instead left her job and flew to the city where Peggy and the man lived. When this other woman arrived, the boyfriend immediately abandoned Peggy and their unborn child. She still vividly remembers the sorrow that engulfed her at this time.

Very concerned about what others would think, Peggy's parents called her to say there was absolutely no possibility she could keep the baby. The baby was illegitimate, and therefore arrangements would be made to have it adopted. They overrode an offer from Peggy's girlfriend to help her keep the baby. Threatened with being disowned if she disobeyed her parents, Peggy gave up her son for adoption when he was born, and most of her extended family never even knew she had had a child.

In the years that followed, Peggy suffered from depression and low self-esteem. She also manifested destructive behavior. At the same time, she continued to look for ways to heal herself and tried various spiritual paths. Because of Peggy's tendency toward introversion, she was uncomfortable reaching out for help or support. She did not trust easily, nor did she have the confidence to establish a relationship with a spiritual mentor.

Peggy moved around quite a bit and worked as a cook. If she shared any of her painful past, it was usually to a paid therapist. When she told friends that she had given up her baby for adoption, she was generally met with blank responses. This further contributed to her sense of isolation, and eventually she repressed her memories and grief.

In her early sixties Peggy decided to search for her son. She quickly found his name through the Internet, and within a few months she was able to confirm his identity and made contact with him. After their initial contact, they began to correspond, but they have not yet met in person. At the same time, Peggy did a lot of reading about adoption and about other women who shared her situation. These stories facilitated her healing process.

Yet even with therapy, Peggy reported that she wasn't experiencing the deep healing she was hoping to find. She still suffered from isolation, a sense of rejection, low-grade depression, shame, and codependency in an unfulfilling relationship with a man. She decided to try meditation and had begun to look for retreats to go to when a friend suggested that she attend a Kapala Training retreat at Tara Mandala.

Peggy began working with her demons of isolation and rejection, and reported that "like a miracle, I immediately felt relief." She continued with the process, and made the connection between giving up her son for adoption and her various emotional issues. Here was the immortal head, the core wound of losing her child, the betrayal of the father of her son, and being shamed by her parents, all of which happened at roughly the same time. The relief and healing that Peggy felt as a result of feeding this demon hydra has given her great hope for the possibility of living a healthy emotional and spiritual life.

Many of us have hydras and will discover surprising connections when we start feeding our demons. The demons we first work with may be only one head of a many-headed hydra. If you discover you have a hydra complex, mapping it out can be very helpful. In making this kind of map you create a drawing with what you see as the core issue at the center, such as sexual abuse. Then you draw other heads or legs coming out of that and name them: "alcoholism demon," "lack of self-esteem demon," "suicidal demon," "eating disorder demon," "control demon," and so on. The purpose of this drawing is to tie together what might seem like disconnected demons so you can see how they interrelate. As you work with newly emerging demons connected to this complex, you can add them to your drawing. The following chapter offers more ideas on creating drawings, sculpture, and "maps" of your demons.

7

WORKING WITH YOUR DEMONS THROUGH ART AND MAPS

Evil in the human psyche comes from a failure to bring together, to reconcile the pieces of our experience. When we embrace all that we are, even the evil, the evil is transformed.

—*Andrew Bard Schmookler*

BY PAINTING with watercolors, sculpting with clay, or drawing with pencil, pen, or pastels, we can depict our demons and use these images in the process of feeding them. Creating a series of images of one demon over time provides insight into the nature of the demon, and into its evolution. Art gives a tangible presence to something that otherwise lives solely in the mind. Art helps to articulate unconscious content arising through the imagination and to bring it into consciousness. It is important not to try to create something for someone else to see, but to let yourself enter undistracted into the creation of the image. Many people have "art demons" that can be triggered by this process—fears that they are not artistic, or "can't draw," which is why it is so important to emphasize that this art is only intended to help us in our own process.

Working with art in feeding our demons can be rewarding, since parts of the demon will reveal themselves more clearly than they would through visualization alone. In addition, creating a visual rendition of the ally and placing it where you will see it frequently is a valuable reminder that you can call on your ally to support you.

Before beginning, prepare your materials. They can be as simple as some felt-tip pens and a journal, or as elaborate as watercolors, watercolor paper, or a canvas with acrylic or oil paints. If you are working with clay, prepare the piece of clay you will use and place it by your side.

DOING THE FIVE STEPS
WITH DRAWING OR PAINTING

Once you have finished step one (finding the demon in your body) and step two (seeing it personified in front of you), and you have visualized all the details of the demon or god before you, begin your artwork. For example, if you've just envisioned a big green lizardlike creature with yellow slit eyes and spiky skin, quickly pick up your demon journal or paper and render it with as many details as you can remember. Close your eyes now and then to recall the demon if you find that helpful. When you have finished the artwork, change places, become the demon, and allow the demon to speak (step three) while you're holding the artwork so that it faces out toward where you are seeing your "normal" self.

Laurel, an architect working in San Francisco, had a demon of anxiety about money. She chronically spent more than she earned, ran her credit cards up to the limit, and was constantly under financial stress. When she spent money, she felt both giddiness and anxiety. She located this demon in the trunk of her body. It was orange-yellow and amorphous. It felt like waves inside her body, giving her a sensation of nausea. When she personified the demon, it became a large, greedy-looking female figure with big hands and feet. She looked at Laurel stubbornly.

Laurel had prepared her watercolors, brush, and watercolor paper before beginning the process. Once she saw the demon clearly, noticing all its details, she began painting. She kept the image in her mind as she was painting, but didn't worry too much about making an exact reproduction. She painted until she felt she was finished, at which point she propped her work up in front of her and asked the three questions: What do you want from me? What do you need from me? How will you feel if you get what you need?

Changing places, she held the painting on her lap facing her "normal" self and imagined that the figure in the painting was responding. The demon said: "I want to control you. I want more stuff, I want to consume." To the second question, the large female figure replied, "I need to feel full." To the third question, she answered, "If I were full, I would feel satisfied and strong."

When this phase was finished, Laurel went back to her original position and dissolved her body into a nectar of strength. She then propped the painting up in front of her and with her eyes closed imagined the nectar was feeding her demon. After the demon was completely satisfied and the ally appeared, Laurel painted the ally, conversing with it as described in step four. By the time she finished working with the ally and completed step five, Laurel had two paintings, which she later hung by her desk to remind her of the process.

WORKING WITH CLAY

This same process can be performed with clay. One advantage to using clay is that you can work with your eyes closed, allowing the form to take shape as you imagine the demon, and then later you can actually transform the clay demon into the clay ally. I like the symbolism of transforming the same substance that was once the demon into the ally. To work with clay, purchase either regular clay from the earth or a synthetic variety. Place it in front of you on a table. Then, closing your eyes, do the nine relaxation breaths and generate the motivation. As you come to the second step, seeing the demon in front of you, keep your eyes closed and begin to work the clay into the form of the god or demon. When you are finished, go ahead with step three. As you become the demon, hold the clay figure and glance down at it as you answer the three questions. After coming back to your original seat, leave the clay figure in the demon's seat. After feeding your demon and seeing the ally, pick up the clay and quite literally transform the demon into the ally by molding the clay into the ally. Then proceed with the rest of the steps. At the end you will have the sculpture of the ally to remind you of it.

Drawing, painting, and working with clay can be very helpful in further articulating and bringing the demons out of the unconscious mind. It is literally bringing them to light. It also provides us with visual reminders of the process.

DEMON MAPS

Making a demon map can be useful in breaking vicious cycles of demons that have been passed from one generation of a family to the next. Many of us can trace our demons back to previous generations, yet we may be unaware of how they are affecting our current relationships, our work environment, our children, and even our grandchildren. It's often easier to see the demons we have received than the demons we have passed on.

To make a demon map, use a large piece of unlined paper; a pad of newsprint is good, but any blank piece of paper is fine. Begin by writing your own name in the middle of the paper. Then in the middle of the upper left portion of the paper write your mother's name. Around it write the names of your mother's parents and siblings, then go as far back as you can on your mother's side.

Do the same thing for your father on the right side. Below your name, write the names of your children and grandchildren. Around your own name, write in the names of people who are or were important to you: teachers, siblings, lovers, husbands, wives, close friends, mentors, coworkers, bosses—whoever you feel is in your relationship web. Note only the most important relationships.

Now begin to record your demons around your name, the demons of your parents around their names, and so on, filling in as many demons as you can. When you are finished, take some time to look at this map. With a colored pencil, circle the demon where it first appeared, for example, with a grandparent. Then draw colored lines through the generations down to yourself, and from there to your children or your employees or others you have "infected" with your demons. Use a different color for each demon. Sometimes the demon changes form over the transfer and, for example, violence from your father might become low self-esteem in you and a behavioral problem in your daughter. Track this line too, with the same color. Imagine these connections are power lines that create electric sparks where they connect. You will probably see a complex web of explosive connections. Then take your journal and write down whatever comes to you as you look at this web of interpersonal demons.

Hydra Maps

When you are working intensively with a particular demon hydra, it can be helpful to make a demon map for just that particular hydra. Again, start with yourself, your maternal and paternal lineages, and so on. Then fill in demons that seem connected to your hydra next to the names of the appropriate people. When you have finished contemplating the map, draw lines between demons and record whatever comes to mind.

Let's say you are creating a demon map of an abuse hydra. Start by placing yourself in the center of the page and then write the names of the abuser(s) above your name; below your name write the name(s) of anyone you have affected as a result of the abuse. Then draw lines out to the side of your name, and at the ends of these lines or legs write the names of the demons that have come from the abuse. For example, above your name might be the name of the relative, teacher, pastor, or therapist who perpetrated the abuse, and below your name will be the names of children, friends, or loved ones who have been affected. Out to the side of your name might be your alcohol addiction, depression, eating disorder, suicidal thoughts, lack of self-esteem, and so on. Record whatever you can think of, even if the links are not direct.

After making the hydra map, spend time with each of your demons, feeding them separately using the five-step practice. When you do this, other demons may appear, and you should fill them into the map. Creating a separate journal for this hydra that includes drawings of demons and allies may be helpful.

Relationship Maps

Mapping can also be valuable if you are struggling with a relationship. Place yourself and the person you are in a relationship with next to each other. Then diagram their family and yours, and see how the demons connect. Someone with a self-hatred demon, for instance, will often connect with a lover who is critical, and someone whose father is an alcoholic will frequently connect with a lover who is an addict. Someone with abandonment demons may well choose a partner who is unfaithful. Making a relationship demon map can help us clearly see the patterns our unconscious keeps us stuck in. Only when we have identified these patterns, making them conscious, will we stop "hooking demons" in our relationships. Again when you are finished, stop and contemplate your map and then draw lines between similar demons. Afterward write whatever comes to you.

Creating a demon map with the help of your therapist can be

useful. Maps are not an essential part of the process of feeding the demons, but they give you a larger context in which to understand your demons and how they connect with present and past relationships. You may also discover collective demons of racism or sexism that underlie demons on the map. We all exist in an interdependent, multigenerational web, and seeing this laid out in graphic form can be helpful in waking up to our own patterns.

Making a demon map is a significant adjunct to our practice of feeding the demons. It puts our demons in a larger context and clarifies the origins of demons that otherwise seem to have appeared only for us. Our hereditary lineages bring us great gifts and also carry their own shadows; making a demon map can help liberate us from aspects of our own history that may be hidden. It also helps us to avoid passing these demons on to the next generation. Demon maps are not intended to blame anyone else for our problems, but to clarify patterns, leading to greater compassion and more open communication between generations.

BODY MAPS

Another useful idea for articulating your demons is to draw a demon body map. Here you will be working with the records you've kept of demon feeding in your demon journal. Begin by drawing an outline of your body on a piece of paper. Then look at the record of your demons and where you hold them in your body, and write in the names of the demons where you found them in step one. You can also add colors and attempt to draw the texture of each demon from step one. For example, Nancy had a demon of overwork and her back often "went out," causing frequent trips to the chiropractor. She drew this as a series of sharp blue shapes, and she wrote "workaholic" next to it. Fill in as many colors and names as possible. This includes emotional as well as illness demons and demons of physical pain. When you are finished, look at your body map and see what insights come to you. Write these in your journal. You can also draw a map of a specific part of your body. Nancy drew a separate picture of her sacrum and lower back and located several demons in the blowup of that part of her body.

The next part of the book will look at how Machig Labdrön categorized demons, then consider various specific demons and how they might manifest in your own life. It includes stories from a number of people who have been using the five-step method to feed their demons and meet their allies, and shows how the practice has affected them.

PART THREE

TYPES OF DEMONS

8

MACHIG'S FOUR DEMONS, GODS, AND GOD-DEMONS

As long as there is an ego, there are demons.
When there is no more ego,
There are no more demons either!

—*Machig Labdrön*

THE NIGHT the future Buddha, Prince Siddhartha, crept out of the palace to seek the answers to his spiritual questions, leaving behind his wife, newborn baby, and his future life as king, he first encountered Mara, the outer embodiment of the forces within himself that would block his path. Siddhartha had arrived at the top of a hill, and looking back he could still see the palace in the moonlight, with oil lamps glittering in the windows. He had resolved to leave his life behind and seek enlightenment, but at this moment Mara appeared.

Mara hovered in the space before him, saying, "Do not go any further. You should return to the palace, and in seven days you will become a universal monarch, king of the whole world."

Prince Siddhartha replied, "*Mara, I know you.* Becoming king of this world is not what I seek. I seek enlightenment and a path to end universal suffering."

By *recognizing* Mara, the prince was able to overcome him, and Mara slunk away into the darkness while Siddhartha continued on his way. But Mara reappeared throughout the Buddha's life, manifesting particularly intensely on the night of his enlightenment.

I find Siddhartha's statement "Mara, I know you" to be a particularly useful key in understanding the importance of recognizing our demons. In the story of the Buddha, Mara actually appeared in personified form, as a shadowy male figure. But later, as Buddhism developed, the maras were identified as inner blockages like emotional upheaval and pride, which inhibit full awakening. Being able to identify our maras (demons) as they show up is the first step in working with them. If we don't recognize them, they will take over unnoticed. Machig Labdrön, who lived a millennium and a half after the Buddha, had her own categorization of four maras, based on those of Mahayana Buddhism. These four categories help to clarify how the forces that block our awakening might appear for us.

I find it helpful to look at the way Machig categorized demons, as well as what she called gods and god-demons, so that we too can say, "Mara, I know you," when our demons appear. Machig identified four main categories of demons: outer demons, inner demons, demons of elation, and demons of egocentricity. Generally these four categories give us a way of seeing demons—and our work with them—as a progression, with each category taking us deeper into our own mind. Although Machig's categories of the four demons move from outer ones to more and more subtle demons, when we're working with our demons, things may not necessarily progress in this way. You might start with an inner demon like shame or depression and then discover outer demons like addiction connected to these inner demons.

These four categories are not meant to guide us in looking at our demons in a particular order, but rather to give us an overall picture of the way demons can be seen — from external manifestations in which we blame others or are reacting to situations, to more subtle inner levels culminating in the demon of egocentricity, which is the hidden core of them all.

Each category is subtler than the last, so outer demons are the most obvious. These outer demons seem to come from the external world, and they include illnesses, specific fears, addictions, relationships, and family demons. We take a step deeper when we travel from outer demons to inner demons, for now we're working at the level of the mind. Inner demons of anger, anxiety, shame, or depression can function without any external stimulus.

Once we have seen outer demons and identified inner demons, we run the risk of becoming puffed up by our spiritual success. Demons in the third category, demons of elation, stand as a warning about the potential pitfalls that lie in wait for all of us who seek success, whether spiritual or worldly. Pride in our accomplishments and the ego inflation that may accompany it are demons of elation.

And finally we reach the category of demons that is the source of them all, the very foundation of our experience of the world. This is the deeply held idea that we are somehow separate from what we experience as "other." This is the birthplace of all isolation, alienation, and conflict, and without this demon of egocentricity, no other demons would arise. If no enemies existed, who could we fight? When we address this demon we begin to see through the clouds of everyday suffering to patches of infinite blue sky.

OUTER DEMONS

On September 11, 2001, our entire country watched the attacks on the World Trade Center in shock and horror. While everyone reacted differently, fear was a common state of mind in the following weeks, months, and even years as a result of those attacks. In a sense our whole country has a post-traumatic stress demon originating from this event, although for some people it is much more acute than for others.

When hope or fear or some other feeling attaches to an external phenomenon, whether it's a person or an event, we have an outer demon. The Tibetan term for outer demons translates literally as "tangible demons." Sometimes called demons that block, outer demons arise when we are attracted to or repelled by things we perceive through the senses and fixate on this attraction or aversion. Outer demons are created in relationship to sights, sounds, smells, tastes, people, animals, objects, and events, as well as substances like drugs or alcohol, or diseases. The most precise way to describe an outer demon is to call it a demon that manifests through the senses. Outer demons can be reactions to literal threats like terrorists, stalkers, rapists, or partners who perpetrate domestic abuse. They can come from natural events, such as tornadoes, hurricanes, or tsunamis. Diseases or pain, whether internally generated or infectiously transmitted, are outer demons. Outer demons are also connected to collective demons, such as prejudice, racism, or homophobia.

When working with an outer demon attached to a relationship, it can be helpful to imagine feeding the other person as well as feeding the demon created by our reaction to that person. When I fed my demon of fear of losing my son as part of my divorce, I also fed an imagined form of my husband. If you visualize the actual person you have a problem with and feed them, through that process you may develop empathy for how that person feels.

INNER DEMONS

Outer demons are the most obvious level of demon; as we become more introspective, we notice there are also demons that arise within the mind with no outside input. These intangible demons—our inner demons—are demons that arise from the mind. They are sometimes called demons that run on and on, because of the mind's never-ending stream of thoughts. Unlike outer demons, inner demons are not based on sensory input but include emotions, fantasies, memories, and thoughts—both our conscious thoughts and a steady stream of subconscious gossip that we tune into once in a while but that mostly scrolls by without catching our awareness. Inner demons may be products of the imagination or take the form of a neurosis like paranoia. Depression is an inner demon, as is free-floating anxiety (that arises for no apparent reason). Rage too can be an inner demon, if it arises with no external trigger.

Jen, for instance, had a demon of depression, an inner demon that followed her everywhere. She went on vacation to a beautiful island in the Caribbean but was plagued by depression the whole time. She would have this demon no matter what the outer circumstances were. An outer demon tends to be more specific, like fear of flying. An inner demon of inadequacy might become a demon of fear of abandonment, jealousy, or insecurity related to outer events. Just as Hydra's immortal head remained after all the other heads were lopped off, an inner demon will remain even when all the connected outer demons are gone.

DEMONS OF ELATION

The third of Machig's categories is demons of elation. These demons arise from prominence, achievement, or success that leads to ego inflation. Outer causes include fame and reputation, and the power and attention that stem from them. When these experiences get mixed up with the self-clinging ego, they produce a demon of elation. This demon comes up in both worldly and spiritual contexts. For example, spiritual elation demons are attachments to the experiences that develop in meditation.

When a demon of elation connects to spiritual experiences, our spiritual development is blocked. The demon of elation is not caused by the positive signs themselves, but by the ego inflation that can arise by our becoming *attached* to these experiences. Also in a worldly sense, if you become successful and are surrounded by people bowing and scraping, then you are in danger of developing this kind of demon.

DEMONS OF EGOCENTRICITY

The fourth demon, which lies at the root of them all, is the demon of egocentricity. Whether we struggle with objects, mental states, or ego inflation, it is a belief in our own self-importance that lies at the root of our troubles. In Machig's formulation of the four demons, the demon of ego is the source of the other three demons, because the ego creates the clinging that generates those demons.

GODS AND GOD-DEMONS

As I touched on in chapter three, Machig not only spoke about demons but also about what she called gods and god-demons. Our hopes are our gods. Gods create struggles similar to our battles with demons, except they are attempts to *get* something rather than *get away* from something. Gods are involved with struggles of desire and longing rather than aversion. It is important to distinguish between an inspiration, which triggers positive energy and optimism without great attachment or tension involved, and a god, which is connected to longing for something, or being obsessed with a certain outcome.

For example, you might really want a certain job that will get you a big salary hike. You can already imagine the new furniture you will buy and the vacation you'll take. You've applied for the job and are waiting for a call back. You have great hopes for this job, and a lot of tension is generated around these hopes. You jump every time the phone rings, and waves of disappointment follow when it is not the human resources department calling to tell you you've got the job. This kind of emotion-based hope is a god as opposed to a demon.

Gods are often harder to recognize as problematic than are demons. In our culture we are taught that hopes are good. But really our hopes are often based on fears. Take a moment and think about your greatest hope. What do you really long for? Then think about your greatest fear. Aren't they the opposite sides of the same coin, both of which generate tension? I hope for love, and I fear loneliness. I hope for success, and I fear poverty. I hope for praise, and I fear criticism.

In describing gods and demons, Machig merged the two into a single word, god-demon, indicating that gods and demons are two sides of the same coin, that our hopes and fears are inextricably locked together. A god in this context is something that seems as though it will enhance the self; a demon is something that seems threatening to the self. Machig's point in uniting them is that in dividing all experiences into good and bad, the stresses of wanting and fearing are locked together in a cycle of suffering.

When I was living in Italy and writing my first book, I had to return to Nepal to conduct further research. I had limited time and was stressed about getting everything done. In addition, I had to leave my children at a less than optimal moment. Then everything went wrong on the trip from the beginning to the end. I was leaving from Rome and realized I had forgotten my passport on the way to the airport. I had to race back, grab my passport, and return to the airport, terrorizing even the Italian drivers. In Nepal, I missed the people I needed to see by a few hours. I also arrived without the materials I needed. As things went wrong, the pressure built. How would I get done the work I needed to accomplish? I got more and more stressed and in the end achieved very little.

When I finally returned home, I went to see my teacher.

He asked, "How was your trip?"

I replied, "Terrible! Everything went wrong from start to finish. It was exhausting, and I didn't even accomplish what I went to do. What do you think is going on?"

He looked at me and quietly said, "Maybe too many hopes and fears?"

Sometimes we can get caught in a god-demon cycle even about something like a vacation. If we have too many hopes and fears attached to it, even something that is supposed to be relaxing can turn into a nightmare. We try to control every moment and make reservations to stay in the perfect hotel or dine at a top-rated restaurant, but nothing works out. At other times, when we have a looser, more spontaneous approach, magic can manifest in the simplest of things, and one thing flows beautifully to the next without effort or manipulation.

Gods can easily become demons and vice versa. For example, our lover might go from being a god to being a demon and back again. When she or he is doing what we want, we experience a god. When he or she brings up our fears, we see a demon. In a dysfunctional relationship, we cling with longing to the god even though the demon is what we are usually confronted with.

A workaholic may shift between gods and demons as well, clinging to the praise and energy he gets from the work in one moment, and driven to exhaustion by it the next. We might have a fear of illness locked into a desire for health, leaving us always shifting back and forth between hope and fear.

Addiction is a good example of a god becoming a demon. When first we use a substance like cocaine, it seems to enhance everything: our work performance, our sexual experiences, and our relationships. It makes everything better. We invest great *hope* in it, therefore it is a god. "This stuff is the answer! If I just have enough of this, everything will be wonderful."

But soon the god starts to be demanding and it seems as if there's never enough of the drug. The drug starts to have a negative effect on the body. Our nerves get fried, and the drug is pushing us around, making us steal to feed it. The coin has flipped: the god is now a demon. By uniting them, Machig shows us that battling against a demon or pursuing a god are two parts of one dynamic.

So much of our lives is motivated by god-demons: sexual desire (hope of fulfillment / fear of failure to "perform"); workaholism (compulsive desire for achievement / fear of failure); obsession with beauty (longing for beauty / fear of aging). You can always recognize when a god-demon is present, because it is invariably accompanied by stress and tension. Think about your own life. Where do you find hope and fear at the same time? That's a god-demon.

If we were to step out of the dynamic of fear and striving, wouldn't we just end up sitting around, doing nothing? Actually the opposite is true: releasing the tension caused by our god-demons frees up energy, because we are no longer wrapped up in our own hopes and fears. For example, after making peace with a workaholic god-demon, we could still work in a corporate environment, but without the tension.

There's an expression I have found helpful in releasing a god-demon: "Hold it lightly." No matter how much responsibility we have and no matter what terrible or important thing is going on in our lives, if we can internally "hold it lightly," space is created in the situation, and we don't get so caught in the god-demons. Perhaps you can think of occasions when you were able to do things without a great attachment to the outcome and noticed how much better they went and how much more pleasant they were.

Now let's look more closely at the categories of demons, and at examples of how people have addressed them using the five-step practice.

9

DEMONS OF ILLNESS

Thus it became known to all that Mother Labdrön had a
special teaching called "Mahamudra Chöd" that could
prevent 404 kinds of disease and eighty thousand kinds of
obstructions from afflicting them — a most extraordinary
teaching that could establish them in Buddhahood.

— *Sarah Harding*, Machik's Complete Explanation:
Clarifying the Meaning of Chöd

ONE OF the traditional applications of Chöd in Tibet was working with outer demons of disease and epidemics. Those practicing
Chöd would give form to demons by practicing the ritual in
frightening places where there were diseased corpses, such as
cemeteries and charnel grounds. Once they felt the terrifying demons had arrived, instead of fighting them, the practitioners
would imagine their own bodies transformed into nectar that fed
the demons until they were completely sated.

There were spiritual colleges in Tibet that focused primarily
on Chöd practice. The students would study the tradition of
Machig Labdrön in depth for several years and then gradually go
out to frightening places on their own. There was also a tradition,
starting with Machig, of a Chöd pilgrimage to 108 fearsome places

in order to train in the practice of Chöd. Eventually students would become skilled enough to work with epidemics and illnesses as I observed at Apho Rinpoche's monastery when the nuns and monks did Chöd for the sick Tibetan road worker. Not everyone who became proficient in Chöd attended these colleges, but it was an option in certain traditions.

One remarkable result for skilled Chöd practitioners is that they become immune to infectious diseases, and there are many reports of Chöd's effectiveness in Tibet. Whenever smallpox or cholera outbreaks occurred, Chöd practitioners would be called in to help stop them. Not only were great Chöd practitioners able to provide assistance to the afflicted and care for the bodies of the dead without themselves becoming infected, they were reportedly often able to end epidemics by feeding the outer demons of the disease causing the epidemic.

Medically and scientifically diseases are referred to as "distinct disease entities." Contagious disease entities are looking for a way to survive, so they need to "eat." Normally they thrive on, or in, a body. Every time they infect someone, they grow stronger. Most medicine is involved with attacking diseases. The principle behind healing with Chöd is that when diseases are fed by the practitioner, they don't need to consume that person or animal. They are given another place to go for lunch and dinner! This is why in Tibet outbreaks of smallpox and cholera could be stopped with the Chöd practice. The disease entity was being fed through the transformation of the body into nectar, and therefore it didn't need to consume that person or animal.

Although it may seem impossible or miraculous, there is a

real logic to the healing the Chöd practitioners effect. If we can shift our conventional understanding of illness to see it as a form of energy, we can understand this way of healing. I caught a glimpse of how this might work in the West in my experience with Fred.

FRED'S STORY

I met Fred when I lived on Vashon Island, near Seattle, after returning from India in the mid-1970s. I was pregnant with my first daughter, Sherab, and adjusting to the life of a layperson, having recently given up my robes after my years as a Tibetan Buddhist nun. My husband and I would walk across the currant fields and down an old logging trail through the dripping rain forest of redwoods and old-growth cedars to the beach where Fred lived on a farm with his lover. They grew vegetables, made pottery, and kept a milk cow. We bought their fresh milk and then climbed back up the hill to our little house, where we held Sunday-morning meditation groups. Gradually, through this connection, Fred became interested in Buddhism and joined our group. Over the years we became close friends. We lost touch when I moved to Boulder and then to Italy, but many years later, in the early nineties, Fred tracked me down and called.

After we chatted for a while about old friends and what we were doing in our lives, he got to the point: "I have AIDS. I was tested in 1987 and found out I was HIV positive. At that time my helper T cells were pretty high."

"What's normal?" I asked.

"Normal is between eight hundred and eleven hundred, and

mine were eleven hundred at that time. But since then they have been going steadily down. I just got tested, and now they are four hundred seventy-seven. That means I have full-blown AIDS. I'm scared a lot of the time. I haven't been meditating, and my mind is all over the place. I manage a bar, and the hours are terrible. It's a stressful environment. I volunteered for a double-blind study at the VA hospital in San Francisco. It's a study with AZT and a placebo. Every three months my blood has been tested, my T cells are counted and I'm examined for any AIDS-related problems. I hope I'm getting the AZT, but I don't know. The worst thing is the fear. I've watched so many friends die, and it's a horrible process. Every time I get a cold I wonder, is this it? I worry that I'm not getting enough sleep, and I'm not doing much because I'm afraid to get tired. I have to work, and the stress of that worries me too."

The fear in Fred's voice was palpable. Fortuitously, I was going to be in California teaching Chöd a few weeks later. I suggested he come to the retreat. I didn't think the practice could possibly help turn back a killer illness like AIDS, but I was pretty sure it would help with his fear.

Fred decided to come, and when we met the first night of the retreat, I saw his long blond hair had been cropped short and was now streaked with gray, but the twinkle in his eyes and his sense of humor were the same. After we had begun the retreat and I'd taught the process of feeding the demons, he asked if he and I could work together as partners in the practice of feeding demons. I agreed, looking forward to some one-on-one time with him, since I had been busy with the retreat.

When we sat opposite each other, I asked if he'd worked with the HIV demon yet. He laughed and said, "No, it's too big. I can't do it. It feels like it's everywhere. I'm afraid I'd be overwhelmed by it."

I said, "Fred, the big ones get bigger by not being faced. It's more overwhelming when you don't meet it than when you do."

I encouraged him to work with it, and finally he agreed to try. The following is his story, in his own words.

"When I found it in my body, it was all over, kind of a green slime that was sucking on me. When I put it in front of me and gave it a form, the HIV demon was huge. It was shaped like an amoeba, greenish but becoming more yellow at the center, where it had a big mouth. It was close—filling the entire periphery of my vision. I felt a lot of discomfort about bringing up this demon, as well as lots of anger and resentment about having him in my life.

"When I asked what he wanted, he said, 'Everything, including your life. I want all of you, but I want your life slowly. I want to see you grow thin, sick, and weak until you are debilitated and become ugly, and finally I want you to die.'

"I suddenly understood that the demon wanted me to fear it. It wanted to consume me with fear. I realized it needed to feel the power it got from my fear. In response I offered this demon power in the form of my body, one part at a time: my strength, my ability to take care of myself and work, my blood, my skin, hair, eyesight, mind, and so on. With each offering I came closer and closer to realizing that if I gave up my eyesight, for example, I was not my eyesight. What defines me? Who is Fred? What is this me? In giv-

122

ing the demon power, I came to realize the emptiness of this body I've been so attached to. In that letting go, I had glimpses of luminous awareness. Emptiness-awareness. At about that time the demon got dimmer, and it finally disappeared, making me realize it was empty too. I rested in that space of 'no me, no demon.' I continued feeding this demon, daily at first and now every so often. I notice that if I feed it regularly, it is small when I call it up, and if I wait too long between feedings, it gets big again.

"After over two and a half years of feeding this HIV demon, it has become small and faint. I don't think about HIV and feel fear. I don't even think about HIV every day, except when I drag him up for feeding. I don't have much fear of it. Now I have other demons that want some attention. HIV isn't the only demon on the block, as I had originally hoped!"

A year and a half after he started the Veterans Administration study, Fred found out he was getting the placebo and not AZT. He was taking no antivirals and was on no special diet. But after he started feeding his HIV demon, the nurses and doctors monitoring the clinical trial noticed his T cells were going up quickly. In most cases, once they go down they sometimes stabilize, but rarely do they climb again. But they did in Fred's case, and his T cells have remained in the low normal range for all these years. When these doctors and nurses asked Fred what he had been doing, he said, "Oh, just a little meditation." They said, "Whatever it is, keep doing it!" He did, and he is now living in a retreat center in California.

I have seen the five-step practice help many people with serious diseases like cancer, eating disorders, allergies, chronic pain, fibromyalgia, ulcers, and high blood pressure, just to name a few of the demons I have met in myself and others. After Fred fed his AIDS demon, all the energy that had been stuck in his fears of AIDS became available to him. He is no longer obsessed with fear, which was the most debilitating part of the illness for him. The energy tied up in the fear of AIDS is now being used in his spiritual practice and generating compassion for all beings.

FEEDING THE BODY'S MESSAGE OF DISEASE

As we saw in Fred's story, feeding the demons of disease can have remarkable and concrete results. Conventionally, visualizing the disease entity of AIDS as a being and feeding it to complete satisfaction would be considered useless. But Fred proved it could be highly effective. Normally we fight the demons of disease. As soon as we get sick with the flu, we think of defenses: vitamin C, immune-boosting drugs, or cold medicines. While none of these approaches is necessarily a bad idea, understanding the message of the disease, feeding it, and finding the ally can be an important adjunct to traditional and complementary medical approaches. We could approach the disease as a message from the body, and then in the five steps allow it to speak to us.

If we always treat the symptoms by trying to suppress them and never understand what the disease is trying to tell us, we may miss important information that the body is trying to communicate. The brain and the immune system are continually communicating with each other, often along the same pathways, which may explain why visualization influences health. When you think about it, the illnesses that invade our bodies also have a kind of personality. Bacteria and viruses each have identifying qualities and shapes that can be seen under a microscope. A certain cancer is "aggressive" and another "slow-moving."

In the Tibetan language, a demon that causes disease is called a *gonpo*. When we get sick we can feel the invasion of this gonpo. I remember lying in bed recently when I was coming down with the flu and quite literally feeling the virus invading my body. In order for us to "get" an illness, it has to be able to find in us a receptive environment, like a key fitting into a keyhole. Health practitioners might call this keyhole a "depleted immune system" or "genetic tendency." Fear of the disease can also create a keyhole for the disease to slip through. Stress, fatigue, poor nutrition, genetic predisposition, and lack of exercise also create an environment conducive to invasion by a disease demon.

Candace Pert, a former research professor in the Department of Physiology and Biophysics at Georgetown University School of Medicine and a specialist in immunology, has extensively researched the links between mind and body. She discovered that consciously setting an intention or creating a visualization can affect the PAG (periaqueductal gray), located between the third and fourth ventricles in the brain, which is filled with opiate receptors and is a control area for pain. As Pert puts it, "While much of the activity of the body, according to the new information model, does take place at the automatic, unconscious level, what makes this model so different is that it can explain how it is possible for our conscious mind to enter the network and play a deliberate part." Her view is not that the mind has power over the body, but that the body and mind are one; the appropriate model is not that of a king governing subjects, but rather of intelligence distributed democratically all over the body. Both the central nervous system and the immune system possess "sensory" elements—they both are able to receive information from the environment and other parts of the body—and they also possess "motor" elements that carry out an appropriate response.

One example can be found in the digestive system, which is lined with nerve cells and other cells that contain neuropeptides and receptors. (This may be why we have "gut feelings," and also why indigestion affects our moods.) Viruses use the same receptors as neuropeptides to enter the cell. So if the receptors were being occupied by, say, norepinephrine, a neurotransmitter thought to flow when a person is happy, there would be fewer receptors available to the virus to enter the cell.

If we take this dynamic and apply it to our five-step practice, we could say that by offering nectar to the demon or virus, we are creating an alternative way for it to feed; when the virus is being fed through the five-step practice it will have no need to attach itself to the cell receptor and enter the body. Once again, if we think of diseases as "beings" with personalities and needs, we are giving them an alternative way to get their needs met. The entity of the disease is being redirected to another food source and being satisfied, and therefore diverted from feeding on the body. This takes place through the intelligence of the body-mind complex.

In the 1980s, Lydia Temoshok, a psychologist at the University of California at San Francisco, demonstrated that cancer patients who suppressed emotions such as anger had much slower recovery rates than those who expressed their emotions more readily. Temoshok also discovered that immune systems were stronger and tumors smaller in those who expressed their emotions.

We all have cancerous tumors growing in our bodies at any given time, and when we're healthy we all have natural killer cells that keep these tumors under control. These killer cells are controlled by peptides in the body and brain, whose flow is linked to emotional expression. If emotion is not being expressed, then the peptides that are needed to coordinate the killer cells that control cancerous growth may not flow easily enough to do their work. David Spiegel of Stanford University has shown that being able to express emotions like grief and anger can significantly affect the ability of cancer patients to survive.

By feeding our demons we move the energy in a more conscious way than we can by just expressing our emotions. Pockets of blocked or withheld emotions are invited to speak, which moves them more purposefully. If we consciously give form to the signals we are getting from the body as a result of pain, illness, or emotions, then natural protector cells will flow more easily. This is the activation of the ally in the healing process.

Considering all this helps to explain how the process of feeding the demons could be effective with illness. When these demons are left unconscious or suppressed, the body is unable to get its message through, which results in ever more powerful disturbances. Constant stress leads to a breakdown in the immune system. At first the messages from the body might be more frequent colds, but when not addressed, this breakdown might lead to heart conditions or other serious stress-related illness. Feeding the demons provides us with a tool for listening to and nurturing the needs of our intelligent body before we find ourselves in irreversible illness.

Feeding the demons can also be applied to chronic pain. Because little things made her so angry, Linda, a thirty-seven-year-old chef, had been in therapy for two years. Linda provoked quarrels with people, so she was often changing jobs. She developed back pain, but she ignored it. Then, while she was on a beach vacation with her mother and daughter, Linda's back pain got much worse.

After this vacation her therapist, who was trained in the five-step process, suggested Linda feed the demons of her pain, and she agreed to try it. Linda's pain was black, slimy, and cold in her body. The demon was an octopus with many arms that wanted to suck at her head. He had red eyes and didn't want to look at her. By identifying with him, Linda learned that he wanted to feel relaxation and freedom. She felt she was not able to give this to him, because she wanted to keep the little freedom she had for herself. But she was able to give him compassion and love. The demon became friendlier, and his sucking stopped. The pain changed into a prickling sensation.

A few days later the pain returned, and again Linda imagined the demon and offered him her love; this time she was more generous, and after a few more days the pain was gone. She also decided to address the lack of relaxation and recreation in her life and started to take a yoga class and scheduled time off in nature. She made her health a priority instead of driving herself so hard.

When her back pain would begin, she would listen and feed her demon. Her anger decreased, and she was able to catch it as it arose instead of giving in to it.

FLESH-EATING DEMONS OF DISEASE

We might consider the category that Machig calls flesh-eating demons as a primitive superstition, but think about anorexia, tuberculosis, leprosy, and cancer: aren't these flesh-eating diseases? Of course these aren't flesh-eating demons in the ghoulish sense of the term, but diseases that quite literally consume the flesh certainly can be experienced as invading demons. Feeding the demons of these diseases can illuminate factors and underlying needs that ordinary treatment will miss entirely. Let's look at two of these "flesh-eating demons."

Demons of Anorexia

This eating disorder is becoming epidemic among high school and college girls, and more and more young men are affected as well. Anorexia often begins with dieting and binging in cycles, and then accelerates to strict starving, excessive exercise, and use of laxatives. In extreme cases, which are sadly not uncommon, the body quite literally eats itself, first the fat, then the muscles, and finally the organs. In anorexia, the most common cause of death is congestive heart failure, which occurs when the heart is consumed until it can no longer function.

There are no reliable statistics for eating disorders because so many people are ashamed to talk about them, and doctors often treat related illnesses without recognizing they are caused by eating disorders. We do know that they are on the rise, that there are reports of girls as young as five with eating disorders. Statistically, 20 percent of those diagnosed with eating disorder illnesses will die of them. The demon of anorexia often has to do with control and perfectionism, as well as with cultural pressures on girls to be superthin. Anorexia also comes up in girls with the onset of puberty as a way to control the uncomfortable changes in their developing bodies.

Jamie was the oldest of three children and had always been the one her mother could depend upon when the going got rough, as it often did with her stepfather. Her mother would confide in her so much that sometimes Jamie felt like she was the parent instead of the child. She started dieting when she was about eleven, after her stepfather commented on her budding breasts. Humiliated by the looks he gave her when she entered puberty, she was afraid to become a full-bodied woman. She had a strong will and found she was successful at dieting. This gave her control over something in an unstable, frightening environment.

Jamie started to starve herself. Gradually she lost more and more weight until, when she got down to ninety-four pounds, she finally was hospitalized by her mother. She tried various methods to recover, but nothing worked for long. She would always go back to starving herself. When she was twenty and had left home and was going to school, she heard about the practice of feeding your demons through a friend, who recommended a lecture I was giving in California. She came and then decided to attend a retreat.

Weighing only a hundred pounds and on the verge of dropping out of school, Jamie had all the signs of starvation and anorexia. Her limbs were just bones covered with skin that had a soft fuzz growing on it, a sign of anorexia. Her eyes were bright and glazed. Still, she mustered the strength to confront her demon of anorexia.

Jamie's demon looked like the witch in the story of Hansel and Gretel — thin, angry, and cruel. The witch looked at Jamie with a demanding, imperious stare. When Jamie became her demon, it told her she must not eat, saying it wanted to control her. Instead of feeling powerful, as Jamie had expected, she felt insecure. The witch said what she wanted was control, but on questioning she admitted that she needed a feeling of reassurance and safety.

As Jamie fed her, the witch began to fill out, her wrinkled face became smooth, and she gradually took on a curvaceous body with long flowing hair, like a Greek goddess. This goddess was the ally. She told Jamie she would help her to accept her body and to let go of control, and this would allow her to relax. She would help Jamie stop trying to be perfect. Jamie realized afterward that when her mother had gotten involved with her stepfather and their world had started to veer out of control, food was one thing she could control. And not eating also protected her body from developing into an object of desire for her stepfather.

Jamie drew a picture of the goddess and started consciously doing what her ally wanted, instead of always being hyperresponsible and controlled. She began to realize that some things were beyond her control and others were not her responsibility.

She began to dance for fun and spent more time in the forest and at the ocean near her apartment in Southern California. This brought her into her body and made her happy. Jamie continued to work with the demon of anorexia with a therapist, gradually letting go of her addiction to perfection and beginning to trust and enjoy her female body. She gained weight and, although the witch sometimes comes back, Jamie now knows how to work with her: she doesn't obey the witch's commands; instead she feeds the witch and asks her ally for help.

Cancer Demons

Cancer is a demon that affects thousands of people. There are many kinds of cancer, and feeding this demon can be a very helpful contributor to your healing process. Rose, a health professional who often advised others about their health, was shocked when she herself was diagnosed with breast cancer. She opted for chemotherapy and radiation and began an intensive process of treatments. But it wasn't working; the cancer was spreading. She had practiced feeding demons before, but she didn't think to try it again until she realized the chemo wasn't working.

When Rose brought her attention to her body and into the breast that was affected, she found a hot, red stickiness. When she conjured it up before her, she found a raging young girl. She asked the three questions and changed places. The girl was furious and, answering the first question, said, "I want you to stop and listen to me. Why have you been neglecting me? You stupid idiot, you keep hiding me. I'm going to get you. Don't you know I'm stronger than you?"

In answering the second question, about her real need, the

red girl replied, "Stop pretending that the abuse didn't happen! I hate the way you ignore me. I hate you!"

A rush of shame came over Rose. She remembered that as a little girl she had been molested by her uncle, but she thought she was "over it" and didn't want to bring it up in her family because she was ashamed and felt it was her fault. Her uncle had also threatened to say it was she who seduced him if she "told." She had decided to forget about it, tell no one, and repress any memories that came up. When the red girl showed up, everything fell into place.

The red girl continued. "I need a voice; I need to communicate. I don't want to be silenced. I won't be silenced. I'll make you suffer if you silence me anymore."

When she responded to the third question, about what she would feel if she was listened to, she said, "I would feel loved."

Rose felt nauseous, not just from the aftereffects of the chemotherapy she was undergoing, but also from what she knew to be true. That night, while doing the five steps, she fed the red girl her love and attention. She also got out a set of watercolors and her paints and painted her demon. It was scary, but she felt better after she had finished. Seeing the image in front of her helped her to connect with the demon and interact with it, anchoring its form and its voice. She also painted her ally, the figure of the Greek goddess Aphrodite.

Rose decided to perform a five-step process and create paintings every day, putting the paintings up on her walls. She left her paints out so it was easy to do, and she found the painting was relaxing as well as clarifying. Over the next few weeks, the red girl became less angry and sad. Eventually she became a soft and sensitive child wearing a red dress and holding a little stuffed bunny like the one Rose had had as a child. Rose also painted her allies, who appeared in various forms.

After a few months of this, Rose was tested with CAT scans and told her cancer was in complete remission. She left some paintings of the demon and her ally on the wall as a reminder, and she continued to feed this demon whenever fears about her remission came up. She also continued with chemotherapy and radiation treatments and has entered psychotherapy to work with her abuse issue.

In looking at the demons of disease we can see how feeding instead of fighting disease can be effective. Even in less dramatic situations, when you feel as if you are coming down with a cold or flu, for example, try feeding these demons. Sometimes giving the surrounding emotional issues a chance to speak will stop the illness. In cases like these, you may have multiple demons to work with.

Even if you decide to fight your disease with remedies, traditional solutions, or conventional medicine, discovering the underlying needs of your disease demon can help stimulate new insights. And the ally that you find in the fourth step may be helpful in giving you support during treatment.

10

DEMONS OF FEAR

Confess all your hidden faults!
Approach that which you find repulsive!
Whoever you think you cannot help, help them!
Anything you are attached to, let go of it!
Go to places that scare you, like cemeteries!
Sentient beings are as limitless as the sky,
Be aware!

—Dampa Sangye (1045–1117) to Machig Labdrön

SOME FORM of fear is common for most of us. It may be a crippling phobia, post-traumatic stress syndrome, or something less dramatic, but most of us have some fear demons. Statistically, one in ten Americans has specific irrational fears. There are many demons of fear that involve avoidance of certain situations or objects: fear of public speaking, fear of the dark, fear of dogs (or cats or spiders), fear of heights, fear of water, fear of flying, fear of highway driving, fear of contamination, fear of abandonment, fear of death, fear of poverty, fear of being raped, fear of cancer, fear of blood or injections, and fear of failure, to name just a few. Agoraphobia, a fear of open space or of any place where escape might be difficult or help unavailable, is another common fear that affects more than three million Americans.

All these fears are based on the perception that some outer event is "happening to us," that something external is coming to harm or kill us, which tells us that these are outer demons. But the external trigger is dependent on the individual; when a group is exposed to exactly the same experience, one person in the group may react with fear whereas another won't. Fear can come from trauma, it can be "inherited" from a parent, or it can be generated by loss, but often people can't trace the source of a specific fear. Even if you realize the fear is unreasonable and excessive, you may not be able to control it.

Avoiding situations that provoke fear can interfere with your occupation and your social life. Fears can also come out of nowhere and suddenly "attack" you. Fortunately feeding the demons of fear can be very effective. Fears create avoidance, and they often live in dark, inaccessible places within us. By giving them form, discovering the underlying need beneath the fear, and feeding that need, we can liberate persistent phobias and specific fears. Below are a few examples of various kinds of fear and of how people have worked with these demons.

SOCIAL PHOBIA DEMONS

One common and crippling kind of fear is social phobia, which affects more than five million American adults. Social phobia usually begins in childhood and adolescence, and it involves fear of being wrongly accused or misjudged and criticized. This can lead to being afraid to eat or drink while being watched, a fear of public toilets, and reluctance to participate in social situations.

Douglas, a thirty-eight-year-old stock trader, suffered from an intergenerational demon of poor self-esteem and social phobia. His parents, who themselves were both physically and emotionally abused, passed on to their son their own feelings of low self-worth. Douglas overcompensated for his feelings of inferiority and weakness by generating feelings of superiority and arrogance, making himself feel safer. His mother suffered from depression as well, and because Douglas felt responsible for her happiness as a child, he never wanted to share his own negative experiences with her for fear of making her unhappy. As a consequence he never learned to process negative emotions.

Douglas gets triggered by meeting new people, public speaking, and being in confined spaces with other people where there is no escape route. He tries to hide his fear and anxiety so that others will not know what he is experiencing, so shame is involved as well. When his demon strikes he has panic attacks, suffers from an inability to breathe in a relaxed manner, sweats profusely, loses his voice, and has intense feelings of impending doom. This social phobia has affected his life by making him want to avoid situations that trigger his symptoms. He has tried to control all social situations to avoid provoking an attack, and has also abused drugs and alcohol to relax in social situations. As a result of his phobia, Douglas has suffered a great deal of anger and frustration for many years.

He knows that a sure way of getting through social phobia is to force himself into difficult situations and learn that once the panic subsides everything is okay. This helps him to see there was nothing to really fear in the first place. As part of his effort to work with his social phobia, he decided to quit his job and come as a volunteer to Tara Mandala, where the demon-feeding process is taught. Because there are many group retreats at Tara Mandala, people come and go often. Though he had to meet new people at each retreat, which he knew would force him to deal with his social phobias, he also knew he would be in a supportive environment.

Just arriving at Tara Mandala brought up his demons in a big way, since he didn't know anyone there, and Douglas developed extreme anxiety. But instead of using alcohol to deal with it, he immediately found a partner and was guided in feeding his demons. Feeding his demons has helped him "meet" the fear within a safe environment, which has in turn given him further courage to face more difficult social situations. After feeding a demon connected to a particular person, he has been able to talk to the trigger person about his fears when the feeling arose. Also, his ally supports him in these direct confrontations, and imagining her by his side helps Douglas feel less alone. He knows it's going to take a while to fully transform these deep-seated anxieties, but in the meantime he is quite happy that he is approaching fearful situations on a regular basis without drugs or alcohol and that his situation is gradually improving. A few years ago, confronting these fears would have been completely out of the question for him; but by using the five-step practice, he has trained himself to meet his fear directly.

FEAR OF LOSS

Miriam suffers from fear of death and loss. She is a mother of three and a practicing rabbi who works in various hospitals as a chaplain. Her father was an alcoholic who struggled with depression. He tried to show his children that he loved them, yet he was often angry and brooding. His own father was also an alcoholic, and beat his children. His mother was reportedly quite remote and unaffectionate with her sons.

Miriam is of course very aware of the tragedies that have beset Jews throughout the centuries. When her brother died suddenly at age thirteen, she took on from her parents an almost pathological fear of losing a child, linked with collective Jewish fears of loss and death. Her core fear is of her children dying.

As she began the process of feeding this demon, Miriam located the sensation of fear in the center of her heart. This was a feeling that included terrible tension and was fiery, orange, sharp, and incessant. In the second step she envisioned the feeling as a huge, bristly Nazi figure, wearing the cap of an SS officer. He was prickly and had a bright orange body. He had many arms, which all held guns and other weapons. His face was furious, with dark, penetrating eyes darting everywhere. He seemed to be psychotic and completely irrational. He wanted to eat and destroy her children. He wanted to eat and destroy all children. But when she asked him what lay below this desire, she discovered to her surprise that he needed security, home, and parents. Then he would feel safe and nurtured.

Having received this information, Miriam transformed her

body into a thick, sweet, milky nectar of safety and security. She poured it all over the demon, repeatedly bathing him. Slowly the demon became smaller and smaller. Eventually he transformed into a child, then a naked infant, helpless, soft, pink, and plump. He slowly got even smaller, and finally dissolved into pure golden light.

When Miriam invited the ally to appear, it arrived as a winged angelic figure. Somehow she knew that this was the Shekina, the female aspect of God in Judaism, the "breath of God." She was about Miriam's size, with long, dark flowing hair. She had deep, loving eyes, fair skin, huge white luminescent wings like a butterfly, and white robes. She promised always to be with Miriam, never leaving her alone, and promised to protect Miriam by giving her strength, wisdom, and resourcefulness. She pledged to always be there for Miriam's children too, providing them with protection and courage.

Sometimes our fears of loss are about the future rather than anything confronting us in the moment; we project ourselves into an imaginary scenario that may never happen and get scared years in advance of a potential event. Dana's mother, Georgia, like her mother before her, is a very intelligent, vibrant, successful woman. Dana herself is a professor with a doctorate in history, a mother of two children, and is active in her community. But she is inordinately afraid of aging. Georgia, Dana's mother, was in her early seventies when she started being "forgetful." Now in her late seventies, she has been diagnosed with Alzheimer's disease. She struggles with conversations, cannot remember what she has read, and has suffered various personality changes. Dana, who lives two thousand miles away from her mother, visits her several times a year. She is not only afraid of the changes she observes in her mother; she also fears what this bodes for her.

Dana decided to work with this fear of aging and Alzheimer's and found it in the pit of her stomach. It felt like a heavy bowling ball of ice. It radiated cold light yet was dead. It almost made her nauseous. When Dana personified the demon, it became a giant man almost eight feet tall. He was blue-white, cold, and very stupid. He had dull eyes and a thick, heavy body. He was like the village idiot, lonely and sad. He moved heavily, without purpose.

Becoming the demon, Dana looked back at herself in bewilderment. The demon wanted to feel normal. He needed companionship and love, and if he got this, he himself would feel warmth and affection for others.

When Dana tried to feed him, she had difficulty but persevered. The demon wanted to be wrapped in a warm white shawl of love, so she did this and then fed him a thick nectar of love and warmth. He raised his head and slowly drank. Bit by bit the demon became smaller, still wrapped in the warm white shawl. Eventually he morphed into a young woman, then into a field of daisies. A young girl appeared, skipping happily, picking a bouquet of flowers. Dana asked her if she was the ally, and she replied that she was not. Then a large white bird appeared. This was her ally. The bird promised to help Dana with her mother, reassuring her and reminding her that we all will die and it will be okay. She has found feeding her fear demon to be very helpful and no longer has a fear of aging.

POST-TRAUMATIC STRESS DISORDER DEMONS

At the end of 1999 I had been attending a month-long retreat in Bhutan, and due to a previous commitment I needed to leave immediately afterward, whereas the rest of the group would continue to travel for a few more days. The Himalayan kingdom of Bhutan has only one main east-west road, and that road is torturously winding, with cliffs on one side and a steep mountainside on the other. I left eastern Bhutan for the airport at 4:30 AM with a guide and a driver. To do the drive in one day was already almost impossible, and then, as we pulled out, the guide told me that the driver had not slept but had been up all night with the local people celebrating the end of our retreat. After an hour or so the driver stopped to wash his face in a mountain waterfall. I looked at him and realized he was exhausted.

Shortly afterward we were going around yet another tight turn when I noticed we weren't turning with the road. We were heading straight for the edge of a cliff. I glanced at the driver and saw he was asleep. I shouted, but it was too late. We were already in the air. The jeep rolled down a steep, forested embankment, flipping again and again, hitting trees along the way. The impact was incredible, punctuated by terrible thuds and the sound of breaking glass.

When the jeep finally came to a stop, everything was dark and I couldn't figure out where we were. Then I realized we were upside down. I tried moving my limbs and discovered I was not seriously hurt. I found the door, got out, and helped the driver and the guide who was accompanying me. They were cut badly in places, and the guide had a dislocated shoulder, but we were able to crawl back up the embankment to the road. There we were eventually picked up by our group and taken to a hospital four hours away, checked out, and then released. After this traumatic experience, whenever I was on serpentine roads with precipitous drop-offs, I would feel nauseous, grip the door handles, look only at the floor, and at times even had to get out of the car and walk.

I have been feeding this demon of fear, and I am gradually healing. When I work with it the demon takes different forms, so I just go with whatever comes up. Once it was a tall, black, iron-spike-covered male figure with sharp teeth. He needed me to listen to him; he needed to feel heard and to control me. If he could be heard he would feel powerful, so I fed him power. When he was fed to complete satisfaction, he dissolved into a puddle of black reflective water, and I rested in the space that remained.

A demon of post-traumatic stress disorder is a specific kind of fear demon produced in the wake of a traumatic experience or series of experiences. Post-traumatic stress disorder (PTSD) affects 5.2 million adult Americans and nearly one-third of war veterans. The numbers of people with PTSD are increasing with the recent upsurge of terrorism and war, and with unusual weather patterns that are prompting terrifying events like hurricanes and tidal waves.

The symptoms of PTSD vary from individual to individual. Some of the symptoms include nightmares, repeatedly reliving the traumatic incident, flashbacks of the traumatizing event(s), emotional numbness, easily becoming startled, irritability, aggression, apathy, feelings of intense guilt, headaches, gastrointestinal complaints, immune system weakness, dizziness, and insomnia. PTSD is a debilitating condition that may affect a person's ability to be in relationship with people to whom they were once close.

Rebecca, a forty-five-year-old yoga teacher from Austria, was on vacation on the island of Sri Lanka in December 2004 when the tsunami hit. She and her husband were sitting on the beach that morning as the water pulled away from the shore. A fisherman near them shouted to them to run. They ran back to their beachside hotel, but the water was right behind them and a motorcycle blocked the door to their room. Rebecca managed to get into an adjoining room, but it started filling up with swirling water. Her husband had gotten into their room and was able to crawl out the back window onto a nearby hill. At the last minute, with the water up to her waist, Rebecca was able to crawl out a window too, and she joined her husband on the hill. They ran to higher ground and watched in horror as people, houses, cars, and motorcycles were washed away.

The whole area was devastated. People they had known were gone or had lost family members. After staying some time to help clean up, they returned home to Austria, but the post-traumatic stress followed both of them home. Rebecca had already studied with me before the tsunami hit, and she came to a Kapala Training retreat in Switzerland about a year afterward, still overwhelmed by trauma.

When she decided to work with her PTSD demon, Rebecca felt the demon of her fear of the tsunami as a strong tension in her whole body. It felt as though she was trapped. She found the center of the feeling in her heart, and found more in a pain in her lower back. It was black, cold, and slippery.

The demon that appeared in front of her was a male giant, gray-black and scaly. He had huge hands, extremely long arms, and deformed feet. He was very aggressive, heavy, and clumsy. His eyes were both angry and sad. The demon needed tenderness, to be stroked and caressed. His heart needed warm breath to be blown on it to make him feel safe; Rebecca offered him a nectar of safety full of tenderness. After being fed, he changed into a sleeping bear with soft golden fur. When Rebecca asked him about being her ally, he hadn't woken up yet, so she just rested peacefully in the fifth step.

Since her fear was so strong, Rebecca repeated the process. The next time, the demon of PTSD appeared as a knight in armor with black eyes and sharp fingernails. After he was fed, his armor dropped to the ground and a small ballerina appeared. She offered Rebecca liveliness, and agility of mind and body. Though the tsunami demon still comes up, Rebecca now has this method to work with. She does so regularly, and it always leaves her in a state of peace. Gradually her waves of fear have been coming less and less often.

Maura not only suffers from PTSD herself, but as a social worker she also sees this ailment in her clients. She lives alone in a house on "high ground" in New Orleans. Having been through Katrina, she has a fear, connected to hurricanes, that nature is now out of control. Although she plans and prepares for natural disasters, there is a deep conviction inside her that everything she loves will eventually be destroyed. It could happen next summer, or the summer after that, but it *will* happen.

Lots of people in New Orleans are living with PTSD from the impact of Hurricane Katrina, and they share a common dread of the next Big One. In her work Maura listens to the stories of survivors and hears about their fears and losses due to Katrina and their worries about other hurricanes, so she is constantly retraumatized.

When Maura worked with her PTSD, her fear demon was in her shoulders, across her upper chest, and through her arms. It pervaded the top half of her torso, the area that she uses to work and swim (out of danger!). It felt wet and was blue-black in color. The demon that appeared in answer to Maura's exploration was a giant, standing in front of her, large, wet, blue, and black. There were white waves all over its body. It was taller and broader than Maura. It was wild, with large thrashing legs and arms, casting waves and water in every direction as it flailed about. It moved constantly and was so huge and heavy that its clumsy dance could have destroyed her and everything around her.

The demon was angry and afraid. He wanted to kill her and everything she loved. He wanted to reduce New Orleans to rubble. He wanted to savage the Gulf Coast and erase all traces of humanity there. He needed respect. If he got what he needed, he would feel calm.

Feeding this demon was difficult because Maura was so afraid of it. Even so, she decided she must trust the process, because none of her other coping methods had worked. She tried different ways of embodying respect and calm. Finally she became a thick white nectar and rained down on the demon. She fed him through his mouth. The demon was ravenous and only slowly got smaller and less powerful, but finally he melted away.

When Maura invited the ally to appear, a small brown bird rose from the ground where the demon had melted away. It was a strong, wise bird. It said it would help Maura by giving her wisdom, and it would protect her by helping her know what to do. It pledged that Maura and her family would survive whatever changes came. When Maura talks to her stressed clients now, she remembers this bird and the calm she felt after feeding her fear. She finds she doesn't get caught in her fear anymore, and now that she is more at peace with herself, she can be a much more valuable resource to her community.

One of the most common PTSD demons is found among war veterans. Leo is a Vietnam veteran whom the Veterans Administration has rated 100 percent psychologically disabled. He entered the U.S. Marine Corps at the age of twenty and served as a combat infantryman in 1968 and 1969.

Leo returned home, was discharged within three days, and was back in college within two months. He began a seventeen-year ordeal with PTSD that was magnified by a car accident in 1977, which left him unconscious for eight days. In 1985 he began attending a regular meeting of Vietnam veterans at a veterans outreach center in Boston to treat his PTSD. He attended consistently for eight years. He then went into private psychotherapy for three years. These treatments seemed to help him, but the symptoms of PTSD remained, and he took several medications to control it. Leo decided to attend a Kapala Training Level I retreat at Tara Mandala. He was reluctant to attend, but decided to try it because his counselor recommended it.

The demon that came up for Leo was a demon of anger, which appeared as a green cobra. It was ready to strike, and it watched Leo with cold, cunning eyes. The cobra wanted protection and needed to feel safe. After this demon was fed the nectar of safety, the ally appeared as a woman with a green cobra in her lap, and then the cobra faded away. The ally offered to help by reassuring Leo and giving him confidence, and it pledged to always be there by his side.

By the end of the fifth step, Leo felt rested and calm. He realized he had always mistrusted his female side and felt he had to be macho. His father was a marine, and there had been a big emphasis on military values in his childhood. Recognizing his feminine side as an ally in healing the PTSD was very meaningful to Leo, and he feels it is helping him to be more integrated as a person and less fearful. With guidance from his doctor, Leo is now off all medications, and he has had few PTSD symptoms since he began feeding his demons; if they arise he uses the five steps to liberate them.

A PANIC DEMON

Fear can arise from less dramatic life situations as well. Inga, a Norwegian, came to a retreat while in the process of applying for a green card. She had just heard that the requirements for legal residency in the United States were tightening. She was happy living in California and was worried she would have to leave. Her fear of filling out the application was such that she was having trouble completing the paperwork. Panic would rise up and block her ability to answer the questions. While performing the five-step practice, Inga located this demon of fear in the front part of her chest, extending up through her throat and into her eyes, and she began to cry.

The demon appeared to her as an ungraspable void with white eyes. It was the embodiment of the immigration service: a white male ghost, cold and unemotional. When questioned, the demon told Inga that he wanted her to acknowledge his power over her. But what he *needed* was for her to apply for the green card without drama. If she would do this, he would feel calmness and simplicity.

After being fed, this demon eventually became a piece of paper with a lot of writing on it. The writing gradually faded until the piece of paper was blank. Inga's ally, a joyful, wise Buddha figure, appeared and laughed at the piece of paper. He pledged to help Inga relax about the green card and to give her the patience to fill out all the paperwork. After just one five-step session Inga was able to complete her green card application with ease.

Inga's case is a good example of how to work with feeding a demon caused by a specific stressful situation, by one isolated fear. This is an important distinction to make, because fear often arises in reaction to a specific event, whereas a phobia is an easily triggered inner demon that may attach itself to a number of fears.

Feeding demons of fear can have an immediate impact, as it did for Inga, or a series of five-step feedings may be needed, but in any case the practice is a very useful tool for working with fears.

The traditional Chöd practice is designed to flush out hidden fear and greet it with acceptance, directly confronting unpleasant or frightening experiences to understand that the source of all gods and demons is our own mind. Urged by the Indian sage Dampa Sangye to "go to places that scare you," Machig undertook a pilgrimage to 108 such places, and in each one she met and fed the different demons evoked by that place. By feeding our ego-clinging selves to our gods and demons, our hopes and fears, we sacrifice the part of ourselves that generates our fears, liberating us to experience freedom in an entirely new way.

11

DEMONS OF LOVE

The minute I heard my first love story
I started looking for you, not knowing
how blind that was.
Lovers don't finally meet somewhere.
They're in each other all along.

—*Rumi (1207–1273)*

RELATIONSHIPS ARE an area where sleeping demons wake up and get busy. You might think you are finished with a certain demon, and then you start a love affair only to have the demon return and wreak havoc. When we fall in love some of our armor comes off, our hearts open, and we are more vulnerable, encouraging demons to come to the surface. Love requires vulnerability, which threatens the ego, so the demons arise to protect the ego; jealousy, insecurity, control, fear, and codependence all may appear.

Being in a love relationship or living with others can be very helpful in terms of seeing aspects of ourselves we wouldn't see otherwise. As Jungian analyst Marie-Louise von Franz put it, "If one lived alone it would be practically impossible to see one's shadow, because there would be no one to say how you looked from the outside. There needs to be an onlooker."

We've discussed how demons of disease look for available receptors in our bodies. In a similar way our relationship demons are also attracted by specific emotional receptors. We unconsciously find a link in the person whom we choose as our lover, and we have an uncanny ability to find lovers with demons complementary to our own, just like finding the right key to a lock. We might as well say "we linked demons" instead of "we fell in love." You can discover a lot about your outer demons by looking at whom you choose as your mate and at what issues come up with that person. Nowhere do we see projections of our demons and gods more clearly. Usually we see the god first as we fall in love, develop longings, obsessive thoughts, or romantic fantasies. Later the demons show up.

The demons that surface in romance may be fears of dependence or of being smothered. They might reflect old wounds. If we've been denigrated or abused, we may find ourselves "in love" with someone who is disrespectful. If we've been abandoned we choose a philanderer. Until we bring these gods and demons to light, they will continue to show up in our romantic partners.

Carl and Kit seemed like the perfect couple; then their demons locked horns. They met at a friend's wedding. Carl was a thirty-five-year-old lawyer, and Kit was twenty-eight and in graduate school for business. Kit came from a family where things were often chaotic, so she longed for stability. Carl's mother had abandoned him when he was twelve, leaving him to be raised by his father and stepmother. At first Carl seemed strong and protective, so Kit felt safe and cared for, just what she had always wanted.

After six months Carl's protectiveness felt a lot more like control. He didn't want her to see her friends or go to her book club. Kit felt stifled and longed for freedom, and Carl had his own god-demons based on his family history. At the thought of losing Kit, he was assailed by irrational fears of abandonment. When Kit wanted more independence, his demon of abandonment surfaced and he wanted to control her even more, which only added fuel to her desire to escape.

When a couple does god-demon work together, projections can be detached from the partner and seen for what they are. Kit and Carl went into couples therapy with a therapist familiar with demon work. They discussed their issues in a joint session, and then the therapist saw them each separately, leading them through the five steps with their demons and gods. Back at home Carl and Kit shared what they were learning and gradually realized how their demons had interlocked. By facing their own demons they were able to take pressure off their relationship, with Carl gradually relaxing and Kit feeling freer. They learned how they could use their allies, and they began to quickly recognize when their demons were coming up and learned to feed them. Little by little, a genuine, relaxed intimacy emerged in their relationship.

RELATIONSHIP-BLOCKING DEMONS

If we have trouble finding and keeping relationships, this is a sure sign that we need to find what demons are at work. For example, a woman may say she wants to be married and have children, but she may have a demon that fears loss of independence, leading her to choose only men with commitment demons.

Connie had a successful career managing wilderness programs. As she entered her thirties, she yearned for a partner and children so deeply that she created a god-demon out of this desire. She longed to get married and was convinced she'd never meet anyone. But Connie's mother had given up a career to have children, and had always been resentful of the kids for keeping her stuck at home. Unconsciously Connie was afraid of turning out just like her mother, so she kept finding herself with partners who fled at the very prospect of long-term intimacy.

Connie finally realized she might have something to do with her inability to find a committed relationship. She then decided to try to feed her demons. After she fed her god-demon of longing and fear using the five-step practice, it turned into a little deer that offered to remind her of her tender, vulnerable side. She realized that this deer represented the possibility that she could keep her strength and still allow herself the vulnerability and closeness that come with relationships. Having met this ally, she found a small deer statue and kept it on her desk as a reminder of what she had learned.

These days Connie has become more open to men who are emotionally available, leaving behind her tendency to fall for unavailable or married men. She has recently met a man who is consciously looking for a lasting relationship and shares her love of the wilderness. They are developing a promising relationship, and Connie's fear of turning out like her mother has not come up.

A variation on this theme is the demon of giving too much "love" to undependable lovers. Sharon, a forty-six-year-old attorney, grew up without a father. When she was a child, her mother worked all day and her grandmother, who was kind and nurturing, took care of Sharon. Since her mother had no partner, Sharon became her mother's emotional support and primary companion. Because she subordinated her own needs to those of her mother, Sharon grew up feeling dominated and possessed by her mother, rather than loved and appreciated for who she was. When she became an adult, Sharon moved away to make a life of her own, but she was hesitant to get involved with anyone for fear of losing her newly acquired autonomy. Years later she found herself wondering why relationships never really worked for her even though she longed for one. A gay woman herself, Sharon tended to develop relationships with women who were straight, and therefore ultimately unavailable. She would give too much in the relationship and end up feeling betrayed.

When Sharon became aware of her tendency to get into relationships where she was giving a lot but not being met in return, she decided to work with this demon. It looked like a large, puffy, inflatable doll of a woman. What the demon wanted was to get Sharon's attention, and what the demon ultimately needed was to feel loved. Sharon was able to feed this demon the love she herself longed for but never seemed to receive from others. After doing this work for some time, she entered a new and satisfying relationship with an available gay woman.

THE GOD-DEMONS OF RELATIONSHIP

Compulsive habits are frequent outlets for relationship demons. When Derek, a thirty-eight-year-old ecological engineer, became involved with Josie, forty, who had her own catering business, he felt ready to let go of his previous pattern of leaving a woman as soon as she became dependent on him. Josie was independent and self-confident, and he was very attracted to her. Derek's mother had been dependent on him and made him into a surrogate lover, so he would often feel rebellious and act out to assert his independence when a relationship got serious. Derek and Josie moved in together, but after six months Derek started looking at pornography on the Internet and masturbating whenever he had a chance. When Josie discovered his behavior and realized its extent, she felt betrayed and threatened to leave him, so he promised to stop.

Derek was dealing with a god of desire and a demon of compulsion. He longed for erotic freedom and was afraid of commitment. During the next month he kept his promise about pornography, but he started having compulsive phone sex as a new fantasy outlet. Again Josie found out and became angry and jealous. This time when he stopped he couldn't get aroused by Josie. Derek's inability to perform without outside stimulation left him feeling confused about the relationship, and Josie no longer trusted him.

Afraid of losing the relationship, Derek decided to go into therapy. His therapist happened to be trained in demon work, so he asked Derek if he'd like to try it. His god-demon of desire and

fear appeared as a green, slimy monster with big eyes and lascivi-
ous lips. It needed reassurance, which would make him feel safe,
but was afraid of being smothered the same way Derek had been
by his emotionally dependent mother. What the god-demon
needed to feel was safety with spaciousness.

After Derek fed this god-demon, it became a wood sprite ally
that promised to accompany him on his outdoor adventures,
which he'd abandoned when he got involved with Josie, since
she didn't enjoy the outdoors. Derek began to feed the demon
whenever his sexual compulsions arose, and he also started going
on solo hiking trips. This gave him a needed sense of independent and allowed a healthy separation from Josie without betraying the relationship. After a while, he no longer felt the need for
compulsive sexual outlets and was again aroused by Josie. Over
time she regained her trust in him, and they were able to deepen
their relationship and find true intimacy.

Another god-demon we find in relationships is the *puer aeternus*
(or in a woman, *puella aeterna*), the eternal youth who wants to
be open to every possibility, never committing, and refusing to
grow up. People with this complex are often involved with youthful, dangerous activities and avoid the nitty-gritty work of adult
life and committed relationships. The god aspects of the puer
long for spiritual highs, travel with no plans, dream of flying, and
often use alcohol or drugs in the search for thrills. The demon
aspect of the puer may get addicted to drugs or alcohol while
looking for the endless high, and may hurt others by not taking
responsibility for what he or she does. Puers often have seasonal

or short-term jobs, date people younger than themselves, and want sex without responsibility.

Aaron came from a large family, and his father felt burdened by the heavy responsibilities of supporting the household. His mother, who had been depressed for a long time, turned to Aaron to take care of her when his father died of a heart attack in his fifties. When he started dating he never committed to a relationship, and he had many one-night stands. When Aaron was in his late twenties, he got a woman pregnant and reluctantly accepted part-time paternity. As he grew older, Aaron still wore youthful clothes and liked to act like one of the gang with his son's friends. Most of the time he insisted on a healthy lifestyle, fasting and doing yoga, but impulsively he would get completely drunk, have blackouts, try to seduce young women, and drive irresponsibly. Around the time he turned fifty, Aaron attended the twenty-first birthday party of his son, got drunk, and flirted with his son's girlfriend so outrageously that the next day his son told him he didn't want to see him anymore.

At this point Aaron finally admitted he had a problem. He came to a Kapala Training retreat to deal with his problem, and when I spoke to the group about the god-demon of the puer, he realized this was what he had. When he began the five-step practice of feeding this god-demon, he found himself face-to-face with his fear of growing old and being trapped. The puer was a centaurlike figure who kept avoiding his gaze and leaping around. After Aaron fed the puer, the ally appeared. The ally was a wild horse who told Aaron it would protect him by "just being there" for him. After working with both the god of longing to be free and the demon of fear of entrapment, he decided he had to get sober. He also realized he was getting older and really wanted a partner, not just a series of brief encounters leading nowhere. He started therapy, and as he began to understand himself, he saw that he could have a relationship without necessarily re-creating the unhappiness he'd seen in his father. He began to change and stopped binge drinking. He found working with his ally through dialogue also helpful. He eventually met a woman who liked to travel and enjoyed the same sports he did, and he was able to make a commitment to her.

PROJECTING OUR DEMONS

Demon work can be very effective in the area of relationships because so much comes up in love, and the result of linking demons can be intense. If you are in a relationship, think about both your demons and your gods. This may give you deeper insight that makes it possible to work with the relationship in a new way. You can also work with feeding your demons with your partner, using the guidelines discussed earlier for partner work. This can bring you closer together and can create more openness, but it can also be tricky. In demon work you expose your most vulnerable places, and if the relationship does not feel safe, it would be better to work with a trusted friend or therapist.

Seeing our own demons and feeding them can take a lot of pressure off a relationship. Since so many demons are brought up in relationships and projected onto our partner, when we do our own demon work we free ourselves to enter into healthier relationships or heal the one we are already in. In relationships we are often attracted to our opposites but then criticize the very qualities we were first attracted to. The strong, silent man becomes the distant husband who is out of touch with his emotions. The joyful, free-spirited girlfriend becomes the irresponsible, shallow wife. The initial qualities we are attracted to often hide demons that don't become apparent until the relationship gets deeper. They may also be projections of a disowned part of ourselves. In doing demon work we may find our own rejected traits in what we see as our partner's demons.

Relationship demons may also link to family demons. My father's critical nature may be something I dislike, so I marry someone I think is a very different kind of man, only to find that he turns out to be highly critical. Then I criticize him for being critical, ignoring the fact that by doing so I am actually being very critical myself! Bringing a personal demon to an interpersonal conflict involves one intimate partner projecting a denied or disavowed part of themselves onto their partner. We see these parts of ourselves as belonging to our mate, and all the while we feed our mate little cues that encourage him or her to act in the way we project. Then we get upset and attack them. So it's a good idea to ask yourself when you are attacking your partner: Is this my own projected demon?

For example, Len and Linda married young, and by the time they were in their forties Len wanted to have other sexual experiences. Instead of being direct about it, he was always accusing Linda of flirting and infidelity. He would also seem to encourage her, asking if she was attracted to this man or that. Sometimes this would get so intense he would back her into a corner, saying,

"Just admit it, it's okay." She began to wonder if perhaps she really was having these feelings. But when he moved out one day, saying he wanted to explore another relationship, she understood that he had been projecting.

The same thing might happen with someone who says they never get angry but is an expert at triggering anger in their spouse, or at goading them to be angry with someone else. These projections are often part of an unconscious pact we make with our romantic partners with regard to demons. You take the anger, I'll take the sadness. You take the optimism, I'll take the pessimism. So when we consider our intimate relationships, becoming aware of projection can be extremely helpful, giving us the opportunity to take responsibility for our own demons. No one knows your demons better than your intimate partner, which makes this relationship both a priceless gift and a special challenge.

12

DEMONS OF ADDICTION

Perhaps everything terrible in us is, in its deepest being,
something helpless needing our help.

—*Rainer Maria Rilke*

ONE OF the world's most prevalent demons is addiction. Being addicted means surrendering oneself obsessively to something, therefore all addictions are uncontrolled (and therefore misguided) attempts to feed our demons. Behind every addiction is a hungry spirit looking for food to nourish the soul.

As we examine demons of addiction, it's important to recognize that the addictive substances themselves are not demons; our attachment to them is the demon. These demons come from our own mind and attach themselves to an outer object. For example, alcohol isn't the demon; the inner need that led to our addiction is. Removing ourselves from the addictive substance (or behavior) won't change things much unless we're ready to work with our demons.

Have you ever been on a diet and found yourself going through the trash in search of that cookie or chocolate that you threw out in an attempt to deny yourself? Lucia wanted to stop smoking and decided she had to separate herself from cigarettes.

She lived in the country, so she threw out all of her cigarettes and then gave her friend her car to prevent herself from leaving. She stayed at home for a week, craving cigarettes but not smoking. However, the minute she got her car back, she drove to the nearest gas station and bought a pack of cigarettes. In order to quit, she would have to free herself from the demon behind her tobacco addiction, not just remove herself from cigarettes.

Some kinds of addiction are fairly obvious; others are subtler, which makes them harder to identify. One way to determine whether you have an addiction is to notice whether or not you orient your life around a particular substance and hoard or protect its supply. Also ask yourself whether your relationship with the substance is damaging to your personal relationships and work life. Some of the more obvious addictions include addiction to food, drugs, prescription medicines, alcohol, tobacco, or cutting oneself. More subtle addictions involve perfectionism, sex addiction, pornography, shopping/spending, gambling, the Internet, work, or exercise. Some addictions have a physiological component, while others are solely based on psychological dependence.

Addiction is often complex, so putting an end to one particular kind of addiction doesn't usually eliminate the presence of addiction in your life. You might stop drinking, for example, but become addicted to prescription drugs because the underlying causes of the original behavior haven't been addressed. Giving up alcohol is the beginning of healing, but it leaves a starving demon that will come out to feed in some other way. The inner demon is exposed once the outer demon is removed, but the inner demon tends to attach itself to another substance to deal with its own unresolved desperation. We need to find the root cause of addiction and feed that demon, or we're just replacing one addiction with the next.

Like any demon, the demon of addiction gains power when you try to repress it. You stop for a while, creating pressure from the frustrated addiction that builds up until it explodes in a binge that's usually worse than the behavior that preceded it. In this scenario it's an all-or-nothing game; there is no balance. Bingeing starts with a quiet voice that protests your repression, insisting that you deserve just one drink, one cigarette, one pint of ice cream, or whatever the substance or behavior may be. Then you have a drink, or a cigarette, and the dam of desire has broken. You want more and more, and if you don't find it, the demon of addiction gets angry. Once you can truly acknowledge the addiction demon by saying, "Okay, I'm going to pay attention to you; tell me what it is you really need," then real healing can begin.

DEMONS OF SUBSTANCE ABUSE

Zoe, thirty-two, is the assistant manager at a large resort. Thanks to twelve-step programs and feeding her demons, she has broken the cycle of addiction, but it was not always so. When she was thirteen Zoe started responding to her troubles at home by cutting herself. At first she did this because she wanted to die, but then it became a way of coping. While she was feeling the physical pain of cutting, the emotional pain would fade, but only temporarily. She discovered alcohol when she was fourteen, which deadened her feelings of self-hatred and despair. She would drink just about anything, without any interest in pleasure or socializing; she just wanted the result. She also discovered drugs and learned that smoking pot numbed her inner pain even more.

Several years later Zoe got involved in a relationship with a drug dealer. As time went on, she used more and more serious drugs. She was sure she wouldn't get addicted to heroin, but within a year she was. She was still in school and had her friends and her family, but she needed the drug too. Although she didn't think she was in trouble, her health declined so much that her parents decided she needed help. Zoe entered rehab, although she still denied having a problem. After she left rehab she decided that she would be fine without heroin, pot, and alcohol. Within a month she was homeless, strung out, and miserable.

Zoe was always looking for something to fill her emotional void. At first drugs and alcohol seemed to do that for her. They gave her some respite from the feeling of emptiness. But she always crashed back into herself and things got worse and worse. She couldn't get high enough to escape herself, but she also couldn't stop. After leaving rehab for the second time, Zoe entered a twelve-step program and began to practice meditation. She stayed clean, but she dove into other addictions—mostly to work and to love—which also became unmanageable. She was still using external things to deal with her pain.

Around this time Zoe's mother heard about the daughter of a friend who was living and working at Tara Mandala. Through this connection Zoe came to Colorado to work for the summer as a volunteer, and she learned about feeding her demons. Her demon of addiction was a gray monster with a vast number of tentacles. Each tentacle had an eyeball on the end of it and was groping around erratically. She realized these tentacles were all aspects of her addiction. Her demon told her that it wanted to be whole so it could stop clutching at things and feel peaceful. This told her that she should feed it peace.

After feeding the demon, Zoe felt calmer, less neurotic, and more confident. As its tentacles shrank and dissolved, the demon became a small groundhog that ran away, leaving Zoe to rest in a state of oneness. Now whenever Zoe craves alcohol or work or love, she feels it in her body as a gnawing anxiety of being "not enough, not good enough," which she sees as the root feeling behind her need to consume. When she explores this feeling in her body and does the five steps, each time the demon looks different and needs slightly different things, but each time she feeds it what it needs. As this process continues, she is finding that the demon returns less and less often.

Addiction to food is also extremely common. Anna, age fifty-nine, ate chocolate compulsively. It gave her comfort and, like an old friend, soothed her when she was feeling vulnerable. Born in Germany just after World War II, Anna grew up without a father, and her mother used to give Anna chocolate for good behavior or when she was going away for a long time. In this way, chocolate developed a deep symbolic meaning for Anna as a surrogate for her mother's love. In stressful or threatening situations, she took refuge in chocolate. She bought large amounts of it and ate it all, leading her to become overweight and to suffer from depression and bulimia. For Anna there was always a moment of hope at the beginning of a binge, as if she might find something in the candy that would satisfy her longing, but by the last piece of chocolate she hated herself.

As Anna started to work with this demon, she found a skinny girl with big eyes who seemed to suffer from malnutrition. Her prominent, resigned eyes said she had tried often to express her needs, but without success; she was hopeless. She needed sweetness, warmth, and security — in short, she wanted to feel a mother's love. Anna fed her nectar of mother's love, and the demon's body eagerly sucked up the energy, becoming a normal, happy girl who wanted to run and play. Anna learned to feed this demon when it arose, and eventually she stopped bingeing. Now that she understood what the chocolate demon really wanted, she could bypass the chocolate and give the demon the love she herself longed for.

WORKAHOLISM

Workaholics stay busy with work and leave little time for anything else. More and more Americans are becoming workaholics, working over sixty hours a week. As with every addiction, there is a compulsive aspect to this behavior, which becomes the primary focus of the workaholic's life. Workaholics neglect their health, their family life, their friends, and their spiritual life, all in favor of work.

Workaholics are not just found in high-paying jobs. Workaholics can be found in any profession, from construction to business to academics. They often accept unrealistic deadlines and don't respect boundaries. For the workaholic there is an overwhelming need to do as much as possible in the shortest amount of time. Workaholics try to control everyone, have difficulty delegating, and put great pressure on subordinates and coworkers. When their health fails from stress and exhaustion, workaholics find themselves alone, with little if anything by way of a social support system.

There's an underlying belief among workaholics that work will provide the big payoff at some point, allowing the workaholic to get out of the game. But this time never comes. There's always more to do. Unlike people who simply work hard, workaholics don't enjoy taking a break, and will often eat meals while working. They always feel as if they are on the clock. Often workaholics are perfectionists who never feel they've done enough.

Those of us with workaholic demons just end up on a hamster wheel of endless striving. Workaholics often leave their children a legacy of depression and anxiety, having placed very high expectations on them, frequently valuing them more for what they do than who they are, and not being available to give them care and nurturing.

Sometimes we make excuses for our workaholic tendencies. Sylvia started a business selling natural children's clothing as a way to make ends meet while she was raising her kids. She was a single mother with two daughters, Abigail and Lisa, so her financial needs were very real. When her business took off, she convinced herself she was still working for her daughters, putting in long hours so she could give them a better life. But the girls were becoming miserable because their mother was too busy to spend time with them. Driven by workaholic demons, she left the children with a nanny, didn't attend school events, and never took time for family vacations. When she became a big success, Sylvia franchised her natural children's clothing concept, which meant she was always jumping on a plane for a meeting.

It wasn't until one of her daughters attempted suicide at the age of fifteen that Sylvia started to pay attention to her life. After buying an audio program at her local bookstore, Sylvia learned about feeding her demons and decided to attend a retreat so she could look into her obsessive relationship to work.

When Sylvia visualized her workaholic demon, it told her that it wanted success and power but its underlying need was to feel peace and harmony. Through all of her striving, Sylvia had always held out the idea that once she got enough money she would feel peaceful. After she fed the demon a nectar of peace, the ally, a beautiful turquoise dragonfly, appeared and told Sylvia that her striving would never end, so she needed to be at peace now instead of waiting. As a result of this demon-feeding practice, Sylvia sold all her stores except the one closest to her home. With the money she freed up she paid for family vacations and was able to work less. She did all of this so she could start enjoying her children again. She stopped conducting business on weekends and began to practice yoga, thus feeding her demon what it truly needed instead of what it thought it wanted. As she continued to feed the demon, her relationship with her children improved. Since then the children have grown up, and they remain close.

Tom had a workaholic demon combined with a power demon. A thirty-four-year-old New York corporate lawyer, Tom always needed to have the last word in any discussion. In social situations he liked to create a feeling of being special by excluding certain people and focusing on those he thought were powerful. He made a lot of money and bought a summer house in the Hamptons so that he could socialize with influential people. He married a New York model for her glamour and her chic friends. He kept long hours and thought about work even when he was trying to go to sleep. At home and on weekends he skipped meals and ate at his computer. He spent little time with his wife, and when he was with her all he talked about was work, never connecting with her deeply and intimately.

Then Tom started to be unable to sleep at night and began to have panic attacks during the day. Around this time his wife realized that Tom had no real love for her as a person, so she decided to leave him. At this point Tom started to feel the walls closing in, so he called a friend he had known from college who had become a psychotherapist. She knew about feeding demons and after hearing about Tom's panic attacks recommended the five-step practice of feeding your demons. At first he was resistant, but in his desperation he decided to try it.

Tom began to work with his anxiety demon but soon found a workaholic demon behind it. When he embodied this demon, he found it was actually weak and vulnerable beneath its veneer of bravado and efficiency. Tom fed his various demons of fear, insecurity, loneliness, and power. He discovered that his panic attacks were actually messages warning him that his life was inauthentic. Since that time Tom has been able to develop a genuine relationship with a woman he met at a retreat, to limit his work to regular hours, and to keep from obsessing about it. He doesn't even log on to his computer on weekends, and he's working on being more open to the feelings of vulnerability that were behind his workaholic demon. Tom no longer has panic attacks, and although he is still successful, he no longer seeks to replace genuine intimacy with work.

As you look at your own addiction demons, find the need under the longing for the substance or the external situation. You will then begin to address the cause of your addiction instead of just its symptoms. God-demons of addiction take many forms, but underlying them all is a feeling that there is something out there that's going to work as a quick fix or numbing agent for the difficult feelings inside. Ironically, the longer we look out there for answers, the bigger our need becomes. Paying attention to what lies under the demon of addiction frees it—and all its related demons—from trying so hard to get our attention.

Addiction is a clear example of how the outer world is not the problem. This is why diets, prohibitions, and repressive strategies have never worked with addiction; they all assume the issue is the substance rather than the person's relationship to it. By feeding these demons and coming to a place of rest and integration in the fifth step, we can treat the insanity of addiction at its root level. When dealing with a serious addiction, I suggest a holistic and integrative approach using psychotherapy and twelve-step programs as well as feeding your demons.

13

DEMONS OF ABUSE

The shadow is the other side. It is the expression of our own imperfection and earthliness, the negative which is incompatible with the absolute values.

—Erich Neumann

ABUSE DEMONS come from internalized feelings triggered by physical or emotional abuse, which is why these demons so often run in families and across generations. It is impossible to estimate the number of people affected by various kinds of abuse, because most of it goes unreported. Yet we must not use lack of statistical evidence to minimize the importance of these demons, for they are some of the most destructive we experience.

There are many kinds of abuse, including, but not limited to, child abuse, emotional abuse, physical abuse, child sexual abuse, date rape, domestic violence, harassment, intimidation, adult sexual abuse, and psychological abuse. Sexual abuse is one of the most common and destructive kinds of abuse, especially when directed at children. Childhood sexual abuse often results in lifelong suffering, which may include addiction, self-destructive behavior, and suicide. Molestation is not always physical; it can include verbal trauma. The same holds true for spousal abuse, a form of domestic violence that frequently involves rape. Abuse is often perpetrated by those in power: parents or caregivers, teachers, professors, pastors or priests, and therapists. Wherever there is a significant power differential in a relationship, there is potential for abuse.

Only recently—and only in certain countries—has child abuse been acknowledged as a serious problem resulting in lifelong damage. In sexual abuse, the pressure placed on the victim by the secrecy, the intense feelings of shame, and the fear of repercussions may prevent children, and even adults who might be aware of the abuse, from seeking help. Sexual abuse involves the double dynamic of sex and power. Pastors, therapists, and teachers have many needy, vulnerable, trusting people coming to them, and they are empowered by the institutions they represent. This can be an invitation for abuse if the person in power has unmet needs or desires and relates to others without supervision. A demon of abuse may initially present itself as depression, addiction, or other self-destructive behaviors, but after these more apparent demons are fed, the demon of abuse comes out.

When a demon of abuse is discovered, I suggest creating a demon map for this particular issue (see page 101). Demons of abuse are usually hydras with lots of different legs and heads. I also suggest working with a licensed therapist trained in dealing with abuse demons, because the emotions they bring up may be intense. You may need the support of a professional to go through this process. Working with the allies that appear is also important; getting specific about how the ally will protect you can be especially healing, because lack of protection from those who should be providing it is one of the traumas of abuse.

Someone who has been sexually abused or molested often has a tendency to disassociate from the body. For this reason, I suggest that in the fourth step, instead of dissolving your body into nectar, you imagine you have the magical ability to produce an infinite amount of nectar to feed the demons. This keeps you "in your body," not disassociating from it as you may have done when you were abused. This method can be used whenever someone is uncomfortable imagining that their body dissolves into nectar. However, the offering of the body should be done when possible, because it is a key piece of what Machig taught as the method of going beyond self-clinging.

Sometimes abuse demons from early in our lives can lead us into further abuse, as in the case of Donna, a good-looking, silver-haired fifty-eight-year-old who manages a bakery. As a child she was routinely beaten by her stepfather, and during her twenties she married a man who re-created her childhood. He traumatized her, keeping her in a state of constant fear for years. When she finally got out of the marriage, her self-esteem and confidence were in tatters. Her trust in men had been destroyed. For the next twenty years she seldom enjoyed male companionship.

Donna decided to work with the demon of her trauma from men. When the demon appeared, she was not surprised to see he was shaped like the international male symbol seen on restroom doors. He had no hands or feet and no features on his head. His trunk was thoroughly encased in clear crystals that stuck out like glass shards. His name was Prickles.

When she changed places with this demon and became him, he said, "I am covered with lacerating shards of quartz, and I am cold. I behave badly. I make sure you reject men. I've been with you for a long, long time, and you hide behind me because you are really afraid. I am big and strong and have power over you. What I need from you is to let me retire. I am so tired of your negativity, and you don't need me anymore. I want to feel peace."

Donna imagined she could produce an endless amount of peaceful nectar, and when she gave it to the demon he took it in a bucket and poured it into a large bathtub. As he got in, the crystals broke off and his body began to bend and soften. He became a healthy, human male, and a particularly gentle, sensitive man who did not arouse fear in Donna. This man was her ally. Donna rested in a space of relaxation and trust. Since feeding this demon, Donna has felt something significant within her shift. She has had the distinct feeling that an uncomfortable presence residing inside her has departed. She feels hopeful that now she will be able to welcome a man into her life.

People who have been sexually abused are often ashamed of it, as though it was somehow their own fault.

Chloe, forty-four, is an interior designer, married, with several children. She was sexually abused by her father as a girl. He made pornographic pictures of her and raped her. She started her demon work after she went through a very unpleasant experience with a man she loved dearly and wanted as a friend. But he wanted a sexual relationship, and their friendship had ended abruptly when it became clear she wasn't interested in romance. She had been inordinately upset by this but didn't realize it was connected to the abuse. She located the rejection by her friend in her left side. It felt numb, very taut in her body, like dried sinew.

When she brought the sensation in front of her, at first it looked like Gollum from *The Lord of the Rings*. Then the demon changed into a "humpy lizard" that just wanted to have sex, with or without his partner's consent. When she asked the lizard what it needed, the lizard said it "just needed to be a man." When asked what it would feel if it got what it needed, it said, "Strong."

Chloe fed her demon nectar of the strength and confidence of "being a man." At the end of feeding him, she flashed on the image of her father walking away with his head down, across a field. She realized this was yet another manifestation of her incest demon. Her father often seemed like Gollum—slithery, smarmy, and, above all, a coward. She saw tremendous sorrow below the surface of the rapist lizard.

One of the unique things about feeding demons is that they may lead you to make a surprising connection you hadn't considered before. Chloe made the connection between the rejection by a friend who wanted something she was unwilling to give and her father, who wanted something from her sexually instead of just loving her. Before she met this demon she hadn't been able to understand why the disagreement with her friend had been so traumatic for her. She also felt compassion for her father's weakness for the first time, although she had worked with this issue in therapy for years. By feeding this demon Chloe learned two important lessons: first, that she could love her father while abhorring his behavior; and second, that her intense reaction to setting boundaries with her friend was linked to needing pure love without sexual demands, something she never got from her father.

Abuse experiences that are not as overtly sexual as Chloe's still can be extremely damaging. Abusive molestation can be energetic, verbal, or involve subtle ways of touching or even staring. This can be confusing because you might think "nothing really happened," but this is no reason for its destructive power to be minimized. Problems caused by these kinds of sexual abuse can be very deep.

Sophia experienced this kind of invasive molestation. A professional healer living in the Northeast, she was touched inappropriately and emotionally invaded by her father throughout his life. He died the year before she came to Kapala Training, so she was still processing his death during the retreat. She suffered from chronic pain in her neck, which sometimes could be quite debilitating. This pain had been with her on and off for many years, and when her neck "went out" she would get bad headaches that radiated into her shoulders. To help with this, she had to go to a chiropractor twice a week for years.

In her own profession Sophia often dealt with other people's energy fields. More often than she would like to admit, she felt invaded by the energy of her clients. When she decided to work with this demon, she wrote in her demon journal, "I felt the demon of invasion. An outer demon, it was located in my stomach." The demon became personified as a seven-foot-tall male with a smug attitude and eyes as black as onyx. He was handsome and self-assured, and he conveyed to Sophia that he would win in the end. The strongest impression that Sophia had of the demon was his sense of entitlement over her.

He told her, "I own you and have owned you for a long time. I always win over you, and that's not changing now. You should stop trying to resist me, because you really don't want to make me angry." The demon's eyes changed to a piercing red as he warned Sophia, and she became very afraid. She started succumbing to an all-too-familiar sinking feeling that her life was not her own. She felt that she was not safe, and that her own vigilance would not be enough to keep her safe. At this point in the demon feeding, Sophia felt hopeless and lost. What was interesting to her was that the demon embodied so many of the same qualities as her father, although she had never connected her neck problem with him.

When Sophia asked the three questions—"What do you want from me?" "What do you need?" "How will you feel if you get what you need?"—she received the following answers once she sat in the demon's seat: "I want Sophia's life force. I need to devour her. When I get what I need, I will feel complete, relaxed, and fulfilled."

Sophia then moved back to her original seat and began to offer the demon nectar of relaxation and fulfillment. The nectar was cobalt blue with pearlescent white in it. Sophia fed the demon for a long time, until it turned the same blue color as the nectar. The demon then broke open in the middle, and out of its torn carapace flew thousands of multicolored butterflies. These butterflies were Sophia's allies. The retreat where Sophia was doing this demon work was taking place in a large outdoor tent with no walls. When the process ended she looked down, and a beautiful yellow butterfly had alighted on her arm! She saw this as an amazing confirmation of the process she had just been through.

After she feeds this demon Sophia's neck is relaxed, and she no longer needs to go to the chiropractor—she can't remember the last time she went. In her own work she carries far less fear of "picking up" other people's energies. And she regularly connects with her butterfly ally by visualizing it and asking it for help or advice.

14

FAMILY DEMONS

Whoever fights against monsters should see to it that in the
process he does not become a monster. And when you look
long into an abyss, the abyss also looks into you.

—*Friedrich Nietzsche*

DEMONS DO not occur in a vacuum; they are often inherited.
Family demons are passed down from one generation to the next.
Some intergenerational demons, such as the tendency toward alcoholism and biochemical depression, are thought to have a genetic component, but they may also be learned from the behavior
of parents or grandparents. (Recent research also shows that ge-
netics can be influenced by emotional and mental factors.) We
know that the tendency for physical and sexual abuse is often
passed from parent to child, as are fears, eating issues, anger, anxiety, pressure to succeed financially, depression, and perfectionism. If we don't make these demons conscious, we may pass them
on to our children. We may tell our children not to do certain
things, such as abuse alcohol; but if we do them ourselves, our
children probably will too.

Tibetans during Machig's time spoke of mother-lineage demons and father-lineage demons. I found this an interesting way

180

to think about the concept of family demons. What demons do I find from my mother's family, what demons do I see came down through my father's family? What demons do I see that I have "given" to my children? We may be aware that our mother had a certain demon, but we may have never thought further back than that or honestly looked at what we have passed on to the next generation, or what demons our grandchildren are manifesting (depending on how old we are, we can look forward as well as back at family lineage demons). Sorting this out can be valuable in gaining compassion for ourselves and for our relatives. For example, we begin to move beyond the fact that our own mother wasn't there for us when we see that her mother was completely undependable. And then perhaps we can come to recognize that we were also not very good at providing stability for our own children. If we can see these lineage demons, then we can also feel less personally guilty and understand them in a larger context.

As we look at some hereditary demons coming down the family tree from either the paternal or maternal line, think about your own hereditary demons. Sometimes with demon work we get a sudden insight into our family history, as happened with Lily.

Lily's mother was sexually abused by her uncle, Lily's great-uncle. He attacked Lily's mother violently, sometimes with knives, and repeatedly raped her. The abuse was extreme and prolonged. At a very young age, both Lily and her sister, Alice, were exposed by their mother to details about the molestation, and these left Lily hypervigilant and scared a lot of the time. Lily was depressed from the fourth grade on. Her demons of anxiety intensified, and by the time she was in graduate school they had begun to interfere with her daily life. She could barely leave her home, and at one point she would not eat for fear of being poisoned. Lily also had reoccurring nightmares, and fantasies about being shot or stabbed in the head and neck, perhaps because her mother had told Lily about being held down at knifepoint by her uncle and raped.

When she worked through the five steps, Lily evoked a demon in the form of a red scaly child with bright blond hair and pointy ears. It was so angry it would not speak. When Lily asked it the three questions, it replied:

"I want you. I have to kill you in order to get your attention. I need your attention and care. If I receive those things, I will feel loved and my anger will dissolve."

Lily fed the little girl nectar made of attention, love, and care. Slowly the girl began to look more human, until she changed into a version of Lily as a four-year-old child. But she was not the ally. Lily's older sister, Alice, appeared next to this child as the ally. Alice had been helpful and protective of Lily when demons of anxiety and depression had gotten the better of her during and after college. This Alice ally promised to help Lily navigate the tremendous feelings of guilt, ambivalence, fear, and sadness that consumed Lily for being the only female on her maternal side to have escaped sexual abuse and violence.

Recent research has indicated that post-traumatic stress can be passed down through parents to their children in a syndrome called secondary PTSD. In this case, the demon of Lily's anxiety masked demons of sadness, guilt, and fear. In the end Lily absorbed both the child who had remained at the end of the feeding and the ally into herself. She felt a renewed gratitude for her sister and heartfelt openness. After the practice she called Alice, and they had a deep, healing conversation about their childhood. Lily also felt very vulnerable, but in a soft, open way. She continued to work with this family demon over time, to very good effect.

Sometimes physical illness may arise from emotional issues linked to family demons. Demon work can help sort out how the illness interfaces with family demons or other emotional components and reveal the layers of demons that may be involved. Often in such circumstances we may need to feed each of the various contributing demons to find relief. Becoming aware of this can be an important step in healing.

Cindy, a forty-three-year-old mother of two, works as a teacher. Her father was an alcoholic, and she too has struggled with alcoholism. She wanted to create the perfect family where everything was orderly, not chaotic and unpredictable as in her own childhood. She came to a retreat after she had been diagnosed with breast cancer and had just finished chemotherapy.

When Cindy discovered she had breast cancer, she already knew she had control issues. For many years she had managed to maintain the illusion that she could control her life, but now she knew she couldn't. Getting cancer taught her that many important things were truly beyond her control, and that the hopeless effort to control everything was just creating toxic stress. In working with her cancer and control demons, Cindy discovered control was also a father-lineage demon; he was very controlling. She wanted to be perfect and held others to the same standard. She was dissatisfied with her husband and was always trying to force him to take better care of himself. This created a lot of tension for her and everyone around her.

Cindy decided to work first with the control demon, rather than her illness, because she felt it was a contributing cause of the cancer. In the first step, as she was searching for bodily signs of the demon, she was able to feel the control demon around her jaw, which she tended to clench. When she imagined the pain in her jaw, it was yellow-red and sharp. But when it took form in front of her, she suddenly had a vision of a yellow, two-dimensional smiley face. She thought, "That can't be it. That's too tacky." Then it morphed into her father's face, and suddenly she was holding his face with her two hands; in that moment she realized that her father was the demon and the transformation all in one.

Cindy had always had battles with her father, and there were many unresolved issues between them. She realized the control demon had its roots in a god-demon: her father. He was a god because she always longed for him, and a demon because she hated him for the problems he caused her.

When she asked the demon that looked like her father what he needed, he said he needed forgiveness, and if given that he would feel love. Cindy turned her body into nectar of compassion and love. On offering it, she could feel the forgiveness flowing and her jaw relaxing. When she was finished, her father dissolved and her jaw stopped hurting. She felt a deep peace and rested there. Cindy also realized that she had been drinking too much in response to the stress of her illness, and right then and there she decided to find help for her alcohol habit. She committed to stop drinking, to stop fighting with her father, and to use therapy to work through whatever anger she still carried around. Cindy understood from this work that her control demon and being angry at her father were literally making her sick, and that it was important for her to stop fighting this battle and to acknowledge they were both caught in the demon's web.

When Joanna began the practice of feeding her demons, she realized she had inherited multigenerational demons from both parents. Joanna was a successful fifty-year-old writer living in New York City, and she was suffering from burnout and a feeling of spiritual emptiness.

Joanna's mother, Helen, was a good-looking woman, very proper, and somewhat puritanical. As a child, Joanna had everything she could ask for materially: dance and music lessons, good schools, travel, and designer clothes. Her family was prominent in the community, and her parents were very concerned with their public image, a message that Joanna quietly internalized. So Joanna grew up being careful about what she did and what she wore. Within the family, her role was to be nice and to perform for everyone.

Joanna was constantly told she should be grateful, that she was very lucky. As she grew up and started to express herself, she wore unconventional clothes, and eventually dropped out of college. Her mother made it abundantly clear that she was disappointed and embarrassed by Joanna's behavior. Joanna was accused by her parents of being ungrateful. She was confused, because while she agreed that she had been given everything, she also felt empty and inauthentic. In dropping out of school she was looking for something authentic to commit herself to, instead of performing for her family's image.

Joanna then moved to New York and gradually developed her writing career; but she found it difficult to get close to anyone. She felt a deep loneliness and guilt but couldn't explain it to herself. Eventually she married, but she was unable to develop genuine intimacy with her husband. She went through the motions and had two children, creating part of what seemed to be the perfect life—until she discovered her husband was having an affair.

After the divorce, Joanna lived alone again, sharing custody of the children with her husband. She threw herself into her work, ignoring her children's emotional needs. As her children grew up she had difficulty connecting with them, and they grew distant. She felt more and more depressed, even though by now she had inherited a lot of money, which only underscored her feeling that she had nothing to complain about.

Joanna began her demon work after hearing about it from a friend, and then she came to a Kapala Training retreat. Through feeding her demons Joanna came to realize she had inherited a "never good enough" demon from her father, who, in turn, had inherited it from his own father. Her grandfather had wanted Joanna's father to be a lawyer and never supported his choice to become a journalist. Joanna's father had become a tireless workaholic, hoping to become so successful his father would finally praise him. However, it didn't work out that way, and her father was still desperately trying to prove his worth when he died of a heart attack in his sixties.

Joanna's father had been very critical of her choice of career. Like her father, she responded to setbacks in life by overworking, and transferred the demon of outer achievement to her children, who tended to stress about their school performance. From her mother she had inherited the demon of "looking perfect" while being emotionally distant.

Through feeding demons of depression, guilt, and workaholic tendencies, Joanna uncovered these intergenerational demons. She worked with the five steps to address the needs of the "disconnected" and "not good enough" demons she had transferred to her children. After feeding these demons she was able to have genuine conversations with her children in which she conveyed to them that just *being* was enough, that they didn't have to be successful and overwork in order to be accepted by her. Gradually they all grew closer together as a family. And Joanna was also able to develop some friendships with women that felt real and honest. As she began to use her wealth creatively to help others in need instead of feeling guilty, her depression lifted.

From this example we can see how demons cross over between generations and also how a demon like a critical or controlling attitude from a parent gets internalized and passed on to the next generation. Although Joanna couldn't do the actual demon work for her children or for her parents, by doing her own in-depth work and feeding both her outer and inner demons, she was able to unravel the tangle of interrelated issues, and her shifts affected the entire family matrix in a positive way.

As we have seen, family demons pass on from generation to generation and may include both female-lineage demons and male-lineage demons. The web of family demons is like the Hydra that Hercules encountered. The demons of one generation may appear in multiple forms in the next generation, or they can skip a generation and show up in a grandchild. Seeing the multigenerational nature of our demons and creating a demon map (see page 100) can give us a wider view of our story and help us put an end to destructive demons that have carried on for generations.

Sometimes we think we are aware of intergenerational demons and we vow not to perpetuate them. But if we haven't fed them they will show up in unexpected places. As a child, Joe witnessed his father beating up his mother. When he tried to come to her rescue, he was beaten himself. Angry and powerless, he grew up and married a sweet, subservient woman, Martha, and had two children, a boy and a girl. Joe was determined not to act like his father. He worked hard and tried to be a responsible parent, but he had never done any emotional work to resolve the issues of his childhood, and he became depressed and drank too much.

Being aware of the pattern of violence from his father's family, Joe tried not to pass it on. Although he didn't become physically abusive, he was verbally abusive and made belittling comments about his wife in front of their children. The children identified with Joe as the stronger parent, so both his son and his daughter learned to disrespect their mother. Martha reacted to the situation by developing a secret dependency on alcohol. She would drink when her husband was at work to cope with her sadness. She felt powerless and became unavailable to her children. She also grew less and less confident of her abilities to function in the world, and more dependent on Joe, while resenting him at the same time.

Their daughter grew up with a tendency to undermine herself, and got involved with a handsome drug dealer. She got hooked on drugs and became a prostitute. Joe's son suffered from depression, dropped out of college, and seemed unable to get his life together. Both children had developed a shame complex, a feeling that they were fundamentally inferior. They longed for approval, which they had never gotten, and suffered from demons of depression and addiction.

Until Joe started to feed his own demons, the demons from his parents kept popping up in his life—and in the lives of his wife and children. Joe and Martha came to a retreat together. She had begun meditation and heard about the Kapala Training retreat while in recovery from alcohol abuse. At first Joe said he was at the retreat just to support Martha, but when he started doing the five-step practice, he got excited by seeing all the links between his family members and many aspects in his life.

He made a commitment to the five-step practice, and so did Martha. Their relationship has become more respectful and, because of this shift and the conversations they have had with their children, the family is gradually becoming more aware of its patterns. Martha and Joe have developed a regular demon-feeding practice, and although the demons are deeply rooted, Joe and Martha are seeing a way out of their suffering. The improvement between them has affected their children too. Their daughter ended her abusive relationship and went into rehab. Their son went back to school and began a satisfying career as a high school sports coach.

When Michael began his demon work he had no idea it was connected to family demons. He had suffered from social phobia since he was a teenager, and he knew it was a hydra demon with many arms and legs. Having worked for more than a decade in marketing, Michael was in a major life transition, having quit his job, and was using his time to work through his social phobia. As a child Michael used bad behavior to become the center of attention. This was a way of getting the love he would otherwise have missed. Recently Michael discovered that many of his fears are also shared by his father, leading him to believe that these fears were conveyed to him at an early age by his father, who himself had taken them on as a result of his own parents and caregivers. Michael worked with his social phobia as a father-lineage demon.

While Michael wanted to be the center of attention, he also found it difficult to socialize in groups. He always harbored secret fears of not being worthy, or of being broken and imperfect. This led him to believe that his ears stuck out too much, or his breath smelled bad, or that his surname was unacceptable and needed to be changed. Michael wrote in his demon journal: "As one fear subsided, it would be replaced by another. Always the theme was that I needed to change something in order to become perfect." This fear resulted in ongoing infidelities, alcoholism, the inability to eat in public, and a frequent impulse to hide.

When Michael found the demon in his body, it was a cold blue sensation in his gut. When he saw it in front of him, it was a thin, ugly blue figure covered with warts. When he asked the demon the three questions and changed places with it, the demon replied that it didn't want anything in particular. What it needed, though, was water and vegetation. If fed these things, it would not feel as exposed or so uncool. It would have feelings of comfort and balance and be more at home and safe.

What Michael found most surprising when he changed places with the demon was that he suddenly felt as if he knew what it was like for his father to be his father. He wrote in his journal how well he understood "the total love that you feel for your child (myself) combined with the absolute fear of rejection by that which you love, which is part of a sense of not being worthy of that level of love. I [Michael] could see how wrestling with this conflict could lead almost to the point of hatred of that which you loved the very most. This led me to a feeling of tremendous compassion for my father, when up until now I had only focused on his frequent rejection of me."

Thinking about our demons in the wider context of our maternal and paternal lineages can help us to track the broader patterns of demons at work in our lives. For example, your mother might have a fear of being fat that she got from her mother, who had been overweight as a teenager and later criticized her daughter for the smallest weight gain. As a form of rebellion against your mother's restrictiveness, you reacted by overeating. Then, unhappy with being overweight yourself, you put your eleven-year-old daughter on a diet when she became a bit plump, which led to her being hospitalized for anorexia at age fifteen. Today she is plagued by issues relating to body image and eating.

By tracking your own patterns you may be able to liberate your demons and talk to your children about what you've seen, asking their forgiveness for passing on your demons. Intergenerational demons encompass many other demons and are often linked to our own demon hydras.

15

DEMONS OF THE MIND

One need not be a chamber to be haunted
One need not be a house;
The brain has corridors surpassing material place.
Far safer, of a midnight meeting
External ghost,
Than an interior confronting
That whiter host.

—*Emily Dickinson*

AS PART of their training, a group of Green Berets was once sent on a ten-day Buddhist meditation retreat to learn about working with their minds. It was a silent retreat, and they were instructed to sit and focus on their breath from early morning until late evening. They were instructed to gently bring their focus back to the breath if it wandered away. If they had an emotion, they were told, simply note it and return to the breath. They were provided three delicious meals a day and a comfortable place to sleep. The center where the retreat was being held was idyllic. At the end of the ten days, when these elite soldiers broke their silence, one of them said, "Man, that was the hardest thing I've ever had to do. My mind would not shut up. What a nightmare!"

Here were these brave men, capable of facing any external foe, brought to their knees by having to sit quietly with themselves. These Green Berets weren't at war, but they were in another kind of battle, with their inner demons. These demons are sometimes called "demons which cannot be controlled," or "demons that run on and on," or more commonly, "intangible demons." Inner demons such as anger, anxiety, or depression come out of the mind with no prompting from sensory input or outside sources.

Anyone who has ever tried to stop his or her mind from thinking understands about the demons that run on and on. Contrary to what we might like to believe, we do not control our own minds. Quite the opposite: we are controlled by our thoughts and emotions. Even the highly trained and disciplined Green Berets were completely at a loss as to how to deal with their own minds. Like the never-ending strip of breaking news at the bottom of CNN on the TV screen, the mind doesn't stop.

These thoughts and emotions do not occur in reaction to any direct outside stimuli, but they can cause us to do all kinds of things. They are connected to what we call neuroses, or inner complexes, and include such demons as anger, anxiety, perfectionism, paranoia, shame, depression, and inauthenticity, although this handful of examples barely begins to represent the vast realm of possible demons that lie within the human mind.

If you have an inner demon of depression, for example, no matter how external circumstances change you will still be depressed. You would be depressed even in the absence of a sad event or loss, like a death. A state of bewilderment in which we just plow ahead unaware, going from one day to the next, is a mind demon of confusion. When you have this demon and can't decide what to do, and you doubt yourself, this is a demon of self-doubt. Another inner demon is obsession, where thoughts and fantasies spin out of control. You could also have a demon of shyness that makes it difficult to connect with other people.

Demons of the mind run day and night, relentlessly. By noticing and identifying these inner messages and the dialogues we have within ourselves, we can become conscious of our inner demons and liberate them. Now let's look at some of these inner demons and how we might work with them.

DEMONS OF ANGER

Anger can come from an interchange with someone, or from frustration with events or objects. For example, someone you're waiting for may have forgotten the appointment, or someone close to you says something hurtful. It can also bubble up out of nowhere, in which case it is an inner demon of anger. Out of the blue we wake up angry, kick the dog, and snap at the kids. Anger is one of the most destructive emotions. A few words of anger can destroy a long-term friendship or sever a family relationship.

Anger can also be directed at oneself and become a tyrannical inner critic or saboteur. In such cases the destructive energy may be acted out in suicidal thoughts, or suicide attempts, or self-destructive behavior. It may also be subtler and lead us to undermine our own success by arriving late for a big interview, procrastinating, or destroying a promising love relationship.

An important point to make here is that we can *manifest*

anger for a purpose without being caught in hatred. In this case we act fiercely but are not caught in the demon of anger; we are not controlled by it, we are using it to trigger change. For example, a political activist could express anger about a situation without hatred for those who may be responsible. Anger can be cold or hot. Cold anger slams the door and closes the heart; it holds on, for years sometimes, and refuses to soften. Hot anger explodes, sprays forth, and burns deeply. It can come and go quickly or be a steady undercurrent that occasionally spews like a volcano. Understanding and feeding our anger demons can be healing not only for us, but also for those in our lives who suffer the consequences of our anger.

Barbara, a fifty-year-old business consultant, came to a lecture on feeding your demons and took part in the exercises I led during the talk. As she was listening she realized she had an anger demon that had complicated all her relationships. I led the group in a five-step practice, and when she looked at where she held anger in her body, she found it over the heart on her left side, extending into her neck. Its color was dark, a combination of maroon and black, and it generated heat. When she personified it, it became a female infant with a beak and many arms, gnashing its teeth. A tear rolled down its face. There was deep sadness in its eyes.

When Barbara asked the demon what it wanted, it said it wanted her to stop ignoring it. When she asked what it needed, the demon said it needed recognition of its existence and an awareness of its essence; this would make it feel loved. When Barbara dissolved herself into a white, luminous liquid of love, the demon baby took it in and rainbow colors sprang up all around it.

Barbara asked this rainbow baby how it would help her, and it said, "I am your tender heart, your capacity to wake up and be fully present. I will remind you that when you get angry you are covering me up." Barbara worked further with this demon, and after some months wrote to tell me she had noticed that she was no longer getting randomly angry. She still struggled with feelings of vulnerability, but she was working through them using the five-step practice.

PERFECTIONIST DEMONS

The perfectionist demon is a relentless self-critic who makes us feel as if nothing we do is good enough. In the presence of a perfectionist demon, we tend to beat ourselves up and find flaws in whatever we do and how we look. Even when we receive praise, we feel so inadequate that we can't enjoy it. A perfectionist demon doesn't allow playfulness or fun; it's a humorless taskmaster. It easily becomes an outer demon of criticism, focusing on the faults of others and misreading the comments of others as criticism. But it is most intensively aimed at oneself. A perfectionist demon makes a "to do" list that is long and exacting, and even when everything is done, it isn't satisfied.

Fiona had a perfectionist demon, and in feeding it she made a surprising discovery. Fiona's mother was a perfectionist, an endless list maker and planner, which Fiona had ascribed to her mother's temporal-lobe epilepsy. Her mother had suffered from uncontrollable grand mal seizures beginning at the age of six. As an adult, Fiona knew that people with this illness were often very rigid; yet as a child, Fiona could only see her mother as cold, demanding, and unpredictable. Fiona had believed that she would not be loved if she was not a really good girl, and this had motivated her to become a perfectionist with strong self-hatred.

Fiona decided to work with this mother-lineage demon using the five steps. She felt her perfectionism in her chest as a sort of cold, stabbing sensation. When she personified the demon, it appeared as an old, skinny woman with gray hair and wearing a gray dress. She was squeezing Fiona's heart, and her eyes were threatening and dark. Fiona knew it was her mother. Then Fiona saw that the demon was shaking, and she knew that the old woman was frightened. The demon told Fiona that she wanted Fiona's love, but she knew that Fiona only loved her grandmother; the demon needed to feel more lovable.

At that moment in the process, Fiona had a realization. She saw a triangle of unmet need between herself, her mother, and her grandmother. Her mother had always felt flawed and unlovable because of her embarrassing public illness, and to compensate she had tried to be perfect. She needed love from Fiona, her daughter, in order to fill that void and make her feel lovable, but her perfectionism kept Fiona at arm's length. Fiona's grandmother had stepped in, giving Fiona the nurturing love she needed as a child, which had shut her mother out.

Fiona felt intense sadness for her mother, and for the fact that they had never been able to give each other the tender love that they both needed. Nor could they going forward, now that her mother was dead. Fiona then fed the demon sparkly golden nectar of being lovable with a spoon. The demon gradually transformed into Fiona's mother when she was a little girl, and this little girl became Fiona's ally. The ally told Fiona that if she could see herself as lovable without being perfect, her perfectionism could be released and everything would be better instead of worse. She pledged to protect Fiona and to remind her that she was lovable in and of herself, without having to do anything at all.

Sonia also had a perfectionist demon, but hers affected her career. A professional violinist in her midthirties, Sonia never felt her orchestral performances were good enough. She'd go over her little mistakes again and again, obsessing about them. She practiced many more hours a day than did her fellow musicians. Although she was an excellent musician, she took little pleasure in it because of her perfectionist demon.

Sonia's perfectionism came from her critical, controlling mother, who raised Sonia without much laughter, generosity of spirit, or physical affection. Her mother never held Sonia or praised her. Even though she excelled in most things she did, at home Sonia was given the message that something was always wrong with her appearance or her performance.

Sonia decided to feed this perfectionist demon, which had dwelled within her as long as she could remember. When she looked at where she held the demon in her body, she found it was everywhere, like tiny teeth gnawing on every part of her. But command central seemed to be in her throat, where the demon appeared to be gray and thick and ugly, like a fleshy tumor. It was sticky, and it blocked her speech.

The demon took form in front of her as a hideous rodent, an enormous rat sitting back on its hind legs, staring at Sonia. It was almost Sonia's size, and behind it was a cluster of baby rats, but the scene didn't feel very maternal. It felt more like a master with her slaves. When Sonia looked the rat in the eye, she was struck by the cruelty she sensed, although she did not feel any fear or animosity. The rat had needlelike buckteeth and glittery black eyes, and very long, sharp claws on all four feet. When Sonia became the demon, she was struck by how differently she felt; as the rat, she felt insecure and needy, feelings that came to her very clearly and vividly.

The rat said, "I have to be better and smarter than you. You can never have more than I have." If it got what it needed, the rat said, "I would feel so powerful and beautiful." So Sonia gave the rat a gold-colored nectar of power and beauty, with the wish that the rat be completely satisfied. It gorged itself, and all the baby rats gathered around in a feeding frenzy. They became fatter and pinker, then rolled over on their backs like little pigs and gradually disappeared. The big rat became very dull and lethargic. Its dark color softened a little as its fur turned into a thick skin. Its teeth and nails fell out and vanished, and it lay on its back as if asleep. It was still a big ugly rat, but not nearly as threatening as before.

Since the rat hadn't completely disappeared, Sonia realized she needed to spend more time with this demon. In subsequent work with it, she stayed with the process until the rat turned into a happy, pink-cheeked human baby that eventually dissolved, and she rested in that space.

When Sonia invited the ally to appear, she saw a fierce woman who said she would keep guard so Sonia could be creative without stressing over perfection. Over the several months that Sonia worked with this demon, she noticed that her perfectionism was lessening, and she was actually enjoying her performances instead of focusing on little mistakes. She made a conscious decision to stop practicing obsessively, and as a result her playing actually improved. Her music was more full of life, and she herself began to feel the same way.

DEMONS OF DEPRESSION

This is one of those demons that can be so pervasive that it is hard to localize in the body. Finding the motivation to feed a depression demon may be difficult too, because depression can be so immobilizing. Such a demon often contains various feelings that are lumped together: grief, anger, hopelessness, despair, and fear may all be present. Depression can be temporary, or it can be a chronic illness so embedded that it makes it hard to function normally. Depression casts a dull blur over everything. We can spend days, weeks, or even years under the control of this demon.

Sometimes depression is an outer demon that comes from oppression, meaning it is specifically linked to outer circumstances, and if those circumstances change the depression is alleviated. During the Taliban regime in Afghanistan, when women were severely oppressed and not allowed to become educated or to practice their professions, there was a nationwide wave of depression and suicide among Afghan women. But when the problem of depression is not altered by a change in the situation that may have triggered it, this means it is an inner demon. An inner demon is one we carry with us no matter what the outer circumstances are. We could be in a beautiful place with wonderful people and still be depressed if we have an inner demon of depression. In the United States, where antidepressant medications are more and more common, approximately 18.1 million Americans (6 percent of the population) suffer from depression.

Depression responds well to the demon-feeding practice because the first two steps help give a specific shape to the problem, which might otherwise remain lost in the state of fogginess and lethargy that so often accompanies this demon. As we clarify this demon's location, color, texture, and defining characteristics, we bring it into a realm where its needs can be addressed.

Jason was the executive director of an organization for unemployed young people. His chronic depression led him to withdraw completely from his wife and his two children. He became quiet and felt disconnected from everyone, to the point that he was almost unable to practice his profession. He described his experience to his therapist as the feeling of having no thoughts, as though his brain were empty. In social situations, he stopped speaking altogether. His therapist suggested he try feeding his demons.

Jason first practiced feeding his depression demon the day

after he and his wife had hosted a dinner party. He had been unable to participate in the conversation, and toward the end of the evening he had felt so lonely and isolated that he had not even been able to listen anymore. Thinking back on the night's events, he felt a lump in his throat, the muscles around his neck and throat contracted, and he was unable to speak. He felt worthless and ashamed. The color that he associated with this sensation was blue.

The demon he saw in front of him was as large as the entire room. It had scaly, blue-green, iridescent skin, and thirty to forty limbs emanated from its body like rays from a star. It used these extremities as arms and legs, but in place of hands and feet they had hard spikes. Its head sat on top of one of those limbs, and its small, calculating eyes looked very coldly at Jason. When Jason examined the demon more closely, he discovered it was pulsating, its extremities undulating in a constant rhythm. When asked what it wanted from Jason, the demon said that it wanted his company and it wanted to get very close to him. When asked what it needed, it said it just needed to be friends in order to feel lively and content.

When Jason returned to his original seat, his therapist suggested he feed the demon, but Jason said he was repulsed by the demon and didn't want anything to do with it. To motivate him, the therapist explained that the animosity between him and the demon had existed for a long time, and that if Jason didn't give the demon something, nothing would ever change. Jason then agreed to try to offer the demon some closeness, but he did so halfheartedly, and he was not willing to offer it liveliness or contentment. Unfortunately the session was then over, so they decided to continue the work next time. Jason's example shows that if you don't understand that feeding your demons doesn't make them worse but releases them, you may have fear or resistance. You have to either understand the theory well enough to trust the process or at least be willing to try it.

During his next session Jason was more open to the process, and when he visualized the demon it looked the same, but it was no longer pulsing. Its cold eyes still stared at Jason. However, as before, Jason did not want to have anything to do with feeding this demon. The therapist encouraged him to try going forward, since nothing he had done up to that point had relieved the depression. Jason agreed to try it. This time, when Jason identified with the demon, it turned out that the demon needed Jason's happiness in order to accept itself the way it was and to develop self-assurance. If it got what it needed, it would feel joy.

When he changed places with the demon, Jason refused to give it anything, as he was still distrustful of the process. But after a few minutes of encouragement from his therapist, he agreed to feed the demon a little joy. Jason saw the happiness as a dark blue, fluorescent light, which he gradually allowed to flow to the demon. The more he let it flow, the more he himself felt touched, and eventually his long-held tears started to flow too. Gradually he saw that the demon was completely satisfied.

At the end of the practice Jason felt peaceful, whole, and at one with the world. He took the blue pillow on which he had visualized the demon into his arms, hugged it, and wept again.

Then he invited the ally to appear. The ally was a blue-green elf who pledged to teach him joy and connect him to nature. At the end of the session Jason felt very open, and his eyes were radiant. At the same time he felt a little disoriented, because this experience had shaken his negative philosophy of life. But in the following weeks he no longer avoided making contact with people, and he felt more connected to his wife and family. His depression receded after several more sessions.

Jason realized that his philosophy of life had been formed by his depression, and he became willing to give it up. He began to share more of his feelings with his wife, and they developed a closeness he had never experienced before. When he felt happy he did not stop himself by feeling unworthy. Depression still overcame him sometimes, but since he learned to do the demon-feeding practice by himself, he was able to use it on those occasions. He was amazed that the depression he had thought would always control him now seemed manageable.

Jason's experience with depression is typical. As I mentioned earlier, when we are dealing with a powerful demon that has really harmed us, there can be great resentment toward the demon, which manifested in Jason's initial refusals to feed it. Offering just a little of what the demon needs can be a helpful way to overcome resistance to feeding demons.

Sometimes depression is passed from generation to generation. Angela, a twenty-year-old who worked as a sales clerk in a clothing store, had a family history of depression. Her sister had bipolar disorder, and her mother and grandmother were both severely depressed. When Angela undertook the first step of feeding her demon of depression, it felt like a heavy black thing pressing down on her head and shoulders, squashing her. It became a black scorpion, walking on cracked ice, cold and insecure. It wanted to hurt people, to tear at their flesh. When Angela switched seats and became the demon, she felt hateful and violent, and she realized how much anger lay behind her depression. The demon said that it needed someone to feel compassion for it, and it was furious because no one ever had. If it was given compassion, it would feel relief.

As Angela began to feed it nectar of relief, the scorpion changed, its hard shell cracking open to reveal a soft, pink body underneath. Eventually it became a sea anemone floating freely in a beautiful aquamarine ocean, completely relaxed. This ally told Angela she would help her and her family by offering love, an ocean of love, to everyone who suffered from depression.

After working with this demon for some time, Angela told me that it might have helped heal her family as well as herself. Her sister, who had always denied her problem, suddenly joined a support group of other bipolar people in her area and started therapy. There is no way to know whether Angela's work was directly related to her sister's progress, but often family matrices shift when one member of a family changes, and Angela felt her work had done just that for her sister.

SHAME DEMONS

If you feel shame and follow it, you will find many other demons, including addiction, power, abuse, and anxiety. When we have a shame demon we long to be invisible but secretly desire the approval of others. People who are shame based feel as if they have a dirty secret they need to hide, even if they don't know what it is. They are afraid their secret will be discovered and revealed, so they also have a fear of intimacy.

Family shame is often unspoken but all too readily absorbed by children's sensitive minds. For example, Celeste, a young woman who grew up poor, was ashamed of where her family lived. When she was a child, she had the school bus driver drop her in front of a nice house, and when the bus was gone she ran behind that house to the trailer where she lived with her parents and sister. Unfortunately this meant she could never invite any friends home to play, and she lived in fear that her secret would be discovered.

Sometimes shame is difficult to name. Celeste didn't know how to identify her demon, but she knew the sickening sensation that arose from it. When she went into her body, she found her demon in her gut, and she had the physical experience of slight nausea. She started tracing this feeling of discomfort, and saw that it made her ingratiate herself to others. Finally she identified her core issue as a sense of shame, a feeling of not being rightfully and comfortably present in her own body.

This manifested in Celeste's life as a need for the approval and affection of others that compromised her personal integrity. She was afraid to face situations in which she might experience rejection or feelings of incompetence or awkwardness. She often felt like she needed to hide. This was not apparent to others, who saw her as a confident, extroverted person.

Celeste's demon of shame was pink and slimy, and it centered in her throat. She saw it in front of her as a salamander-like form. It lacked a spine and was devious, with darting, cagey eyes. It wanted to confuse her and make her insecure. When she asked it what it needed, it said it needed acceptance of its vulnerability; then it would feel loved. So when she returned to her seat she dissolved her body into nectar of loving acceptance. As she fed this wormlike creature, it gradually melted into a puddle. Then she rested in that open state.

Ever since she got at this core demon, things have been different for Celeste. When the sickening nausea comes, she recognizes it and doesn't get so caught up by it. Instead she thinks: "Oh, okay, I'm feeling that shame again. I don't need to resist it, and it won't take me over. I've been here before; I know how to deal with it." She feeds the demon and the shame subsides. Over time, she has found those feelings no longer ambush her in the same way.

Bethany, a thirty-eight-year-old elementary-school teacher, also had a demon of shame. She suffered from such extreme shame about herself that her very existence seemed shameful. As a child she had been given a book about a baby goose named Borka, whose family ridiculed and teased her because she had no feathers. Borka was so different that she could not hide it. Finally her mother knitted her a rough, gray sweater so she wouldn't get too cold, but she was never able to fly. In the fall when the family left to fly south, Borka was left behind in her sweater, hiding in the grass and crying.

In her family, Bethany felt like Borka, like a displaced alien. Her mother would say to her, "Are you *trying* to look as ugly as possible?" As a young woman she was always afraid she looked ugly, was ashamed of her body, and wanted to keep it from others' eyes. When she grew up she was unable to feel part of any group.

When Bethany worked with her shame demon, she found a rough, gray, coarse sensation in her heart. The sensation became a sacklike demon closed at the top, which wanted to cover her and make her disappear. It was totally unsatisfied and upset with her. When Bethany asked it what it needed, it said it needed to be released from a spell so that it could feel free again. On receiving the nectar of freedom, it dissolved like a snowman melting in a sudden hot spell and became a white deer. As her ally, the deer encouraged Bethany to continue to offer compassion to herself in order to break free from the spell of shame.

ANXIETY DEMONS

Anxiety is a fear that something bad will happen in the future, perhaps violence, an accident, or a sudden loss. There are many forms of anxiety, including panic attacks, obsessive-compulsive behaviors, generalized anxiety, and various phobias. Anxiety affects even more people than depression; about 40 million Americans (or roughly 13 percent of the population) have anxiety disorders. Most people who suffer from one kind of anxiety disorder will also have another, and these frequently arise in conjunction with depression and substance abuse. Panic disorders are often linked to agoraphobia or claustrophobia. Some anxiety is linked to outer circumstance, but often it's not connected to any specific circumstance; in this case it is an inner demon.

Anxiety, like depression, is becoming more and more common, and medications that treat it are more and more ubiquitous. We feel anxiety when our defenses begin to break down and our vulnerability is exposed. This can happen when we lose a job or relationship, or when any event occurs that shakes our world. Fear of terrorism, global warming, and the disruption of families, communities, and relationships all contribute to anxiety.

Monica, a forty-two-year-old woman, the director of a library, is married with no children. She grew up in Europe surrounded by art, music, and literature, in a family that frequently traveled. But when she was fifteen her father was diagnosed as a paranoid schizophrenic. When her mother left to be with him in a mental hospital for several weeks, Monica and her sister were alone.

Her father's paranoia was focused on the imagined infidelity of Monica's mother. Her mother became afraid of him, and three years later they divorced. Monica stayed with her mother and, at the age of nineteen, had her first epileptic attack. When she was twenty she left her mother's house and got a degree in library science. When she was twenty-two her father committed suicide. Although Monica continued to work, she began drinking and having indiscriminate sex on weekends. She also started burning herself with cigarettes. At age thirty-five she began practicing yoga and meditation and stopped her destructive behaviors, but she still was experiencing a lot of anxiety and mistrust. During this period she attended a weekend retreat on feeding demons.

Monica carried her anxiety demon in her chest, where there was a very closed feeling, like a brick wall. The energy was tight, cold, and gray, like pieces of glass. When she personified it she saw in front of her a small, dark human being with no gender. It had black hair, was cold and scaly, and its eyes were helpless and imploring.

The demon wanted to destroy Monica, but it said what it really needed was warmth; if it got warmth it would feel love. After Monica dissolved her body into a nectar of love, the demon became lighter, a friendly, sunny, and lovable being. Then it dissolved into formless light that had a pearl-like sheen. When Monica invited the ally to appear, it was a medicine woman with long silver hair, sitting in a forest. This woman promised to protect Monica and become a figure she could call on when she was feeling insecure.

Anxiety can be overwhelming when events seem to pile one difficult thing on another. Paul was already suffering from anxiety and control issues when he lost his job. Recently divorced, he had to find time to be with his children as well as look for a new job. He had a lot of expenses and thought he might have to sell his house. His life felt out of control. He had learned the practice of feeding demons during a Chöd retreat and decided to apply it to his anxiety.

When he went into his body in the first step, Paul found the anxiety right at the nape of his neck, between his shoulders. It felt jumpy and electric, like a live wire. It was cold, like ice, and made him shiver. It created a discomfiting lightness, leaving him feeling disconnected right where his head sat on his torso. When he put the demon outside his body and personified it, it was a writhing mass of metallic blades—sword blades, razor blades, knife blades, and machinery blades—all connected to a central point that spun wildly. It had no face. When Paul asked the demon what it needed, it said, "Freedom from confinement and more air to breathe." If it got more air it could feel relaxed.

As Paul fed it relaxation, the demon's blades melted away, and it slowly shrank into a small steel sphere made up of many carefully riveted plates. It was still shiny, but a beautiful glowing sheen replaced its harsh reflective surface. It bounced around playfully in front of Paul, who felt relief throughout his body. There was new warmth and a feeling of solidity between his shoulders. The demon didn't want to move back into his body and continued to play in front of him. It became an ally that encouraged him to relax.

DEMONS OF INAUTHENTICITY

When Carla, a fifty-nine-year-old writer, was a child, her mother wanted everyone to get along and be happy, both for outside appearances and for her own peace of mind. Unfortunately, however, her parents handled sibling rivalry ineffectively, and Carla and her brother and sister fought all the time. At family gatherings Carla attended as an adult, the three siblings faked family harmony for her mother's sake. When Carla went to these events, she often ended up feeling like a fraud, trapped by the unspoken message to act as if everything was great. She talked to her brother about it, but he couldn't understand why she was so uncomfortable "pretending" for such a short time. Then she felt worse, feeling that her discomfort was invalid and that she should not have such a strong reaction. Although she continued to attend these events, each time she did she felt she was betraying herself. She experienced a deep loneliness at family gatherings and would cry herself to sleep at night. She realized it was an inauthenticity she had always been asked to maintain.

This demon was hard to deal with because it wasn't anything big like an addiction or depression, but it weighed on Carla so that she came to dread family gatherings. She decided to feed this demon. The cold, bluish sensation in Carla's chest emerged as a witchlike figure, with bluish wart-covered skin. The demon wagged her finger at Carla and looked at her accusingly.

The witch told Carla that she needed to be genuine and then she would feel free. After being fed freedom, the witch took the form of a young girl who was wild and strong. As an ally this girl told Carla she would protect her from betraying herself and would help her say no. When the ally was absorbed into her, Carla felt empowered, and the next time she spoke to her sister she said she wasn't going to the next family event. It was scary but liberating. Since then Carla chooses carefully which family gatherings she attends and doesn't feel she has to go just because it is expected.

Karen, a thirty-eight-year-old psychotherapist, had a similar demon she called the "Sunshine Demon." Her parents divorced when she was four, after her mother decided not to take her father's beatings anymore. After the divorce Karen became the sunshine child for her mother: she was the only source of joy in her mother's life. Standing in for her father, Karen became very practical, learned to repair things, and seemed to have no fears. It was only as she grew up and got away from her mother that she allowed herself to explore her dark side.

As a child, Karen was a good student, usually the best in the class, and she excelled at all kinds of sports. Her mother and the extended family were all very proud of her. Then she got tonsillitis and had to stay in the hospital for several weeks. During her recovery Karen got lots of love, care, and presents from her family. After that she developed a pattern of getting sick to get attention and to take a break from achieving. As an adult, Karen still tried to excel in everything she did, and was a high-functioning professional, but she always got sick when she was under pressure.

Karen's five-step practice with this demon began when she woke up one morning with a sore throat. She was taking a new training course and was under pressure to complete a project. She knew her demon always came in the same way: a tickle in her throat followed by a headache and sore throat. It came when she felt pressure to perform but really needed love.

As soon as she focused on her throat, Karen's tension disappeared and was replaced by a warm, open feeling in her heart. She continued and gave the feeling form in the second step and discovered a comic figure whose head was a sun with a smiling face, like a child's drawing. It laughed so hard that she couldn't see its eyes, and it avoided meeting her gaze by dancing around making a show. Watching it made her laugh, it was so joyful.

When she changed places and embodied the joyful demon,

Karen was surprised to find that behind the sunshine mask she felt incredible sadness. The sunshine demon needed to be seen and loved for who she was, instead of for her facade. As Karen sat in the demon's chair she began to cry. She continued to cry when she went back to her original position, because she recognized her deeply ingrained pattern of pretending that everything was fine.

She fed the sunshine demon love and acceptance, and it became a very sweet four-year-old girl with blond hair and ribbons in her braids; but she wasn't the ally. The ally appeared as a fierce yogini surrounded by flames. Afterward Karen noticed that the warm feeling in her heart had spread to her whole body. Her sore throat and headache were gone. From this experience she recognized the burden she had been carrying for her family and how she used sickness to get out of it. Now when she feels that tickle in her throat she does a demon feeding instead of getting sick. When it is possible she does it with a friend; otherwise she does the five steps alone.

As we feed our inner demons we may find issues that we thought would be with us forever abate and dissolve. Sometimes this happens all at once and sometimes it takes a series of five-step practices. In my own life I had to work for a month on my abandonment demon before I noticed it wasn't coming up anymore. Sometimes I still have regressions into it, but for the most part it's gone. When it comes back, I now know what to do.

Inner demons thrive in our thoughts and memories, and as we learn to free them they dissolve like waves falling back into the ocean. The true nature of the mind is clear and lucid, so gradually, after we have fed these demons in the fifth step, we can let the mind rest in its own nature, which is as vast as the ocean. Demons of the mind can lead us to harmful actions like hurting ourselves or others, so it is important to be aware of them. Like the Green Berets who suffered more from their inner demons than from outer enemies, most of us suffer more from what arises within than from what oppresses us from the outside.

16

DEMONS OF ELATION

Man's shadow, I thought, is his vanity.

—*Friedrich Nietzsche*

DEMONS OF ELATION, Machig's third category of demons, have two aspects: attachment to worldly prestige and inflation from accomplishment on the spiritual path. It is important to understand that demons of elation are just as destructive as the more obviously negative outer and inner demons. They are also more difficult to recognize, because they are connected to pleasant experiences. As we've seen, each of Machig's four types of demons takes us deeper into our own mind. Each category is subtler than the last, and this third group of demons—demons of elation—is subtle indeed.

We are always looking for experiences that will give us the ultimate buzz, whether it comes from drugs, alcohol, or other kinds of pleasure like food, sex, or travel. Ironically, the longing for epiphany is itself a kind of spiritual obstacle. I remember attending a monologue by the late Spalding Gray, cofounder of the Wooster Group theater company in New York City, performing in a small theater there. He was describing a trip to Asia in which he spent the whole trip trying to find the single moment of epiphany, which constantly eluded him. In listening to him I realized how much this longing for that one perfect moment drives us, giving rise to gods and demons.

WORLDLY DEMONS OF ELATION

Worldly demons of elation are connected to an inflated sense of pride around success, work, family, or possessions. Think about times when you have felt puffed up about your clothes, your home, your appearance, your car, or your wealth. This demon is also connected to any profession that is held with respect and in which you might have power over others. When I think about this demon, I have an image of someone literally getting inflated like a balloon. The boss who has power over the lives of employees can develop an elation demon, inflated by the praise or status he receives from his job. Inflation can also occur when someone becomes rich, famous, or both, developing a sense of self-importance and of deserving special treatment. Or these demons can be a more subtle pride in one's children or one's professional abilities.

I was talking about this demon with my friend Christine, a doctor. She said, "Ah, there's a period during medical internship when this demon shows up. Doctors who train interns call it 'the dangerous time,' because the interns become overconfident and arrogant about their diagnoses."

She told me about Jody, a bright radiology intern who graduated from Harvard Medical School. She was proud of her ability to read X-rays, so when she saw two unusual X-rays in one session she immediately jumped to a conclusion. But as she reviewed the

X-rays with her supervising doctor, he pointed out that she had overlooked a few important clues and as a result had missed the diagnosis completely. In retrospect Jody realized that her feeling of enormous confidence was a warning sign she had ignored.

SPIRITUAL DEMONS OF ELATION

In discussing demons of elation, Machig emphasized spiritual demons of elation, which emerge when we get attached to the status and auspicious signs that arise along our spiritual path. Like the worldly demons of elation, these are considered tricky because they are connected to positive experiences. Spiritual demons of elation can lead to the misuse of spiritual authority through the manipulation of other people for our own gain.

In the present era of instability and soul-searching, there is a great opportunity for preachers or gurus to use their position to create cults or control other people's minds. If you are a spiritual teacher or mentor, you may be overcome by praise from disciples or devotees who are impressed by your spiritual qualities. You might be offered large sums of money or status. These things can rob you of your humility and lead to ego inflation.

An extreme example of the spiritual elation demons was Jim Jones, an American who founded a cult that moved from the United States to Guyana. Jones considered himself to be a reincarnation of both Christ and Lenin. In 1978, when he was visited by a U.S. congressman investigating potential human rights abuses, Jones ordered the killing of the congressman and some of his party and then forced a mass suicide in which more than nine hundred of his followers died.

These spiritual demons of ego inflation become powerful in cult leaders who are clever at manipulating people with hope and fear. One way you can recognize teachers or ministers caught in this demon is by their delineation of themselves and their mission as good and of the rest of the world as evil or corrupt. These leaders are often sectarian and paranoid. Such leaders can try to prevent their followers from having relationships with the "outside" world, and maintain that they alone can judge the worth of their devotees. They also may believe that violence can be justified to fulfill their mission.

In our own lives this might manifest less dramatically as spiritual pride, the desire to have others think we are spiritually fully realized. Sometimes if we do a long retreat we want everyone to think we are enlightened at the end. If they do get this idea, we are in danger of colluding and leading them astray. It is important to be alert for this tendency in ourselves, to keep relationships with our own teachers genuine, and to continue to practice with diligence.

Although it is important to recognize the dangers posed by spiritual leaders who misuse power, it is also helpful to remember that many authentic teachers are not in the grip of the demon of elation. Often the greatest teachers are the most humble and unpretentious. For example, His Holiness the Dalai Lama is considered to be a living Buddha by the Tibetan people and could certainly be at risk of being caught by this demon, yet he is humble and compassionate to everyone.

If we find we have taken on an air of self-importance, or start labeling those who think differently from us as wrong, this is the demon of elation at work. If we are in the grip of this demon, we stop examining our own motives and actions. Our behavior may become sloppy and careless. If demons like this appear and we fail to recognize them, we will be taken over.

One of the ways we can avoid getting caught by the demon of elation is to be warned about it in advance. Ayu Khandro, a great twentieth-century yogini whose biography is in my book *Women of Wisdom*, was in retreat when nomads came to ask her for help. She says in her biography: "In late autumn, an epidemic broke out among the nomads' animals. I was asked to intervene, which I did with the Chöd. The epidemic stopped and everyone began to say I was a great practitioner. As they began to honor me, I was worried, remembering Trulzhi Rinpoche had said this was a demonic interruption. So I entered stricter retreat." She had been warned about the demon of elation, recognized the potential for it, and protected herself from it in this way.

In a more contemporary setting the demon could come up for teachers or ministers. Chris is a popular professor of Eastern religion at an East Coast college, known for teaching cutting-edge courses. At one of my lectures, when I described the demon of elation, a bell went off for him. He subsequently attended a retreat and confessed that he felt he had this demon. He hadn't yet abused his status as a popular professor, but he recognized a tendency in himself to enjoy the admiration of his students. He saw the potential for abuse of his power. He fed the demon during the retreat and later wrote me that although it had been hard to admit to this demon, he felt knowing about it had helped him avoid abusing the esteem he was offered by his students.

Ayu Khandro, recognizing the risks posed by this demon, applied one of the traditional antidotes: to go into strict retreat, because in strict retreat there's no one to offer applause! Not all of us have the luxury of doing this, so it's wise to be aware of the potential pitfalls of the demon of elation. However, being praised alone is not necessarily a sign of being caught by this demon. If you are honored but recognize that the praise is like a hollow echo, then you are not in the grip of a demon of elation. But if you are praised by your students or colleagues, or attract a large entourage, you are in *danger* of falling under its sway.

Priests, teachers, ministers, yoga teachers, gurus, sheiks, rabbis, or leaders of any religion run the risk of being associated with the divine or the enlightened, which gives them a special power and authority over others. This position as the earthly representative or intermediary of the divine lends itself to the demon of elation. When traditional Buddhist thinkers teach about the demon of elation, they always emphasize its dangers for spiritual seekers.

Another interesting aspect of this demon is how it manifests itself internally. At the inner level it is spiritual pride coming from attachment to spiritual dreams, visions, meditation experiences, or spiritual powers. You might have a special dream and then go around bragging about it to anyone who will listen, or you might have a particularly good meditation session and think, "Wow, I must tell my friends about this. I must be pretty advanced to have this happen." If you get attached to such experiences, the progress of your meditation is blocked and its blessings degenerate. In the Tibetan tradition one of the safeguards against this kind of demon is to share your spiritual experiences only with your teacher. These experiences may be exciting, but it's important to hold them close.

For example, Tamara had an amazing dream in which she was in a cave surrounded by luminous beings, receiving an initiation. Afterward she told anyone who would listen about the dream, and she had a feeling of elation and pride as she told it, believing it showed what a spiritually elevated person she was. Instead of continuing to practice her spiritual path intensively, she decided this was a sign that she had arrived at her goal, so she slacked off on her spiritual practice. Gradually she got caught up in distractions and lost the opportunity to really go forward on her path.

People can also get caught in the demon of elation when using drugs to try to experience spiritual epiphany. Whitney learned about psychedelics in college and began using them with the hope they would take her to the ultimate experience. She did have some amazing mind-opening experiences, but she always came down and needed to take another "trip" to try to get back to that ultimate experience. She never gained insights that changed her life in any significant way, and she kept trying to return to where she had once been, looking for a way back to the door to heaven. Gradually she realized that she needed to develop a real path and stop trying to get her epiphany chemically. So she started a yoga practice, slowly cleaning out her system, and eventually began to go to meditation retreats. She came to a teaching on feeding demons, and when she heard about the demon of elation, she recognized its role in her drug experiences.

*   *   *

The demon of elation can attach itself to both spiritual and worldly situations, and warns us of its presence through grandiosity, overconfidence, abuse of power, attachment, and ego inflation. Anyone on a spiritual quest should know these moments will come and are actually opportunities to go deeper into our path. Becoming caught by demons of elation is like seeing a sign for Paris and thinking you have arrived in Paris. Spiritual experiences and dreams are an indication you are going in the right direction, but they are by no means the end of the path. For those who are on the spiritual path, the demons of elation, whatever form they take, are something to be aware of and guard against, as we saw in the life of the Buddha, when Mara tried to seduce him.

At the same time, we need to guard against the pride and inflation of worldly success, which can cause us to mistreat others and lose sight of our real values.

17

THE DEMON OF
EGOCENTRICITY

The army of the four demons cannot hurt you,

If you harbor not subject-object thinking,

No demons can e're harm you.

—*Milarepa*

WHEN TIBET'S great yogi Milarepa was living in a cave doing a long retreat, the story goes, a demoness decided to test his realization. She enlisted the help of other demons, and one night at midnight they attacked Milarepa full force. At first he was frightened and called upon his guru, the deities, and his protectors to help him. This made the demoness happy, for she felt she had proven he was not realized, and the demons increased the intensity of their attack.

Suddenly Milarepa recalled the teachings on the nature of mind that he had received from his teacher, Marpa, instructions on the inherent emptiness of the self and of phenomena. He was reminded that the power of demons depended solely on ego-clinging. As soon as he remembered this, he shifted his attitude completely and offered his body to the demons in the same way Machig had done with the attacking nagas. Immediately the demoness and her entourage changed their attitude and pledged to protect him and his followers. She also advised him that whenever his mind ran wild he should meditate on the essence of mind and not get caught in ego-clinging. It was clinging to the self that made him afraid, and so the demoness was showing him that understanding the demon of ego-clinging is essential to truly understanding the nature of demons.

In meeting the demon of egocentricity, we finally come to the deepest and most central of all the demons. When I first heard about Machig's way of categorizing the four demons, it seemed to me they were in the wrong order, that the demon of egocentricity should come first, not last. But then I saw that it is the very process of understanding the other three demons that allows us to see the fourth demon.

You will notice that I have included no separate examples of the demon of egocentricity in this chapter, because it is not truly a separate demon; since it is the source of the other three types of demons, all of the outer, inner, and elation demons effectively serve as examples of the demon of egocentricity in action.

The literal translation of the demon of egocentricity is the demon of arrogance. This is a good way of describing egocentricity, because it manifests as a feeling of self-centeredness, that we are the center of the universe and everything orients around us. What the ego wants is neatly stated in what are known as the eight worldly dharmas.

Getting what you want, and not getting what you don't want
Wanting instant happiness, and not wanting unhappiness

Wanting fame, and not wanting to be unknown
Wanting praise, and not wanting blame

Through clinging to our ego, the mind becomes afflicted by all kinds of emotional ups and downs, thoughts are seized upon, and karma is created via the actions that result. The real root problem is clinging to notions of self versus other, not realizing how much of what we consider to be external reality we ourselves project. A simple way to put it is this: where there is egocentricity, there are demons and gods; where there is no egocentricity, there are no demons or gods. We can see the demon of the ego in our reactivity, in being irritated by criticism and inflated by praise, in wanting to accumulate material things, and in being upset when we lose wealth, possessions, or status.

We see this perhaps most vividly in two-year-olds as they grab a toy and scream "Mine!" at the top of their lungs, bashing each other ruthlessly over the head. Although we learn to modulate our fixation on ourselves and on what we want or don't want, the same "me, me, me" still occurs in us, sometimes well masked, sometimes not. The spiritual path is the journey toward letting go of the fixation on "me" and "mine," opening to vast compassion, and offering it to all beings. In so doing, we move beyond the ego's fixation on itself.

What causes the demon of egocentricity? Why aren't we all the compassionate beings we know we could be? In one of his songs, Bob Dylan sings: "Something is happening here and you don't know what it is, do you, Mr. Jones?" It is this feeling that something is happening that you are not recognizing which is at the root of the demon of egocentricity. But where does this feeling of not knowing come from? In Buddhism it is called the basic split. This split is between oneself and the rest of the world, between "I" and "other." It occurs when the spaciousness of our true nature is so roomy, so generous, that we have a desire to explore and revel in it. One way to talk about the formation of the ego is to say that our consciousness starts dancing in the vastness, and soon we are dancing so intensely we lose sight of our relationship with that space and become caught up in an experience of "I." As this "I" starts to experience itself as separate and solid, the infinite tapestry of awareness starts to seem solid too. This is how we form the ego and the state of being fixated on duality. The lack of recognition of our vast and immeasurable true nature is called nonrecognition or ignorance.

In this condition of separation a loss of consciousness occurs, a kind of blank state, and in the wake of this comes apprehensiveness, the feeling that "something is happening here and you don't know what it is" arises. This in turn gives rise to the ego's modes of dealing with the anxiety. We have created the solidity ourselves, and once we're caught in the apprehensiveness, we become unable to experience the original, fundamental state of openness. We don't realize we ourselves are creating this experience moment by moment; we think it is coming from outside.

How does this look in everyday experience? When we first perceive an object, such as a dog running toward us, we see it in an open, nonconceptual way. Then the ego jumps in, and we immediately begin to add something to our perception. Maybe we panic, thinking the dog is going to attack us; maybe we seek to avoid it, thinking the dog will jump on us and get us dirty; or maybe we call it and try to get it to love us. The ego reacts and the spaciousness is gone. This is the function of the demon of egocentricity. We feel separate from each other and from everything else. We feel something is wrong and we try to address that feeling, but we go about it in a way that only creates more anxiety. We judge and pigeonhole everyone and every experience, not allowing ourselves to simply be present.

Let's use swimming in the ocean as a metaphor for our relationship to original spaciousness. We can have many relationships with the ocean: we can struggle against it in panic, we can manipulate it for commerce, or we can relax and play in it. The ocean is vast and spacious, so we might feel distrustful of it. But if we can relax the feeling of separation from the ocean and rest in it, we discover the vastness that has always been there. Now we can float easily and restfully in it, and all anxiety disappears. This is release from the ego. There are many meditation practices for arriving here, and feeding our demons is among them.

Unfortunately our strategies for coping with anxiety usually move us further away from recognizing our essential union with the vastness. We struggle and don't trust it. The ego develops cravings, aggression, and delusion as strategies. These mistaken approaches manifest as our demons, but their leader is the demon of egocentricity. The demon of egocentricity is the *strategizer*. The other demons are the *strategies*.

Since the ego establishes and operates on the principle of self versus other, the ego sees everything dualistically, which places us in a constant struggle to keep ourselves viable; even pleasure is infused with tension. The ego requires constant vigilance, and because the ego's task of complete control is impossible, we always have a feeling things are getting out of hand. When we meditate we are learning to release the ego's grasp.

When Machig was attacked by the army of nagas, she was in the tree resting in awareness, a profound state of meditation. Instead of using the usual strategy of the ego, which would be to fight back in terror, she undermined the ego by continuing to rest in meditation, offering her body as food. In this state there were no hooks for the nagas to grasp; there was, in a sense, no one to attack. Seeing this, the nagas surrendered and became her allies, pledging to protect her. If we look at this story symbolically, the nagas are the forces within Machig's own mind arising out of the unconscious. But she chooses not to engage with these demons and instead offers to feed them. By doing so she liberates herself and becomes even more fully realized than she was before.

Fundamentally all the demons that we have looked at are thought processes that block a state of clear awareness, and they grow out of this demon of ego fixation. The practice of feeding your demons seeks to liberate all these demons and transform the energy caught up in them into positive energy, which we have been calling "the ally." All of these energies—the demons and the allies—emanate from within us. In the fifth step, when we rest and relax in the aftermath of feeding our demons and finding the ally, we let go of the underlying demon, egocentricity.

Most of us do not recognize the vastness of our consciousness, even though it is present right now, behind the thoughts you are having as you read these very words. This is because it is so obscured by the drama created by the ego. The spiritual path gradually uncovers this space, giving us glimpses of it, but the experience is not stabilized until we fully wake up.

A Tibetan teacher once explained this to me through a helpful example. It was early morning, and we were sitting having tea on the top floor of his monastery in Nepal, the sun glowing through the golden curtains. I asked, "What does it mean that the fundamental vastness of mind and the fruit of enlightenment are the same?"

He picked up his teacup and said, "Let's say this is the fundamental vastness of mind, otherwise known as the ground of being."

Then he picked up a piece of paper and covered his teacup. "This paper represents loss of awareness of the ground of being, and the confusion of the ego that comes from that loss." He gestured to the paper and said, "The drama of our lives unfolds on top of this paper, with the ground of being hidden below it. The ground of being is right there, but we don't see it, so we feel anxiety, and wander around trying to resolve that anxiety through craving, aversion, and bewilderment. But of course this doesn't work, because these things take us further and further away from the ground of being, and we get more and more tangled up over innumerable lifetimes."

Then he pulled the paper back, slowly revealing the cup. "This is the spiritual path. Gradually we experience the ground of being, at first just a little, then more and more." He pulled the paper off completely. "This is full awakening, or enlightenment, the ultimate goal." Then he offered me the uncovered cup. "You see, the vastness of our true nature and the fruit of full awakening are the same. The ground of being has always been there, but it hasn't been seen."

All living things have strayed into confusion and are living their own hallucination, from the tiniest gnat to the most complex human being. After the dualistic split is established, the ego forms as a kind of central headquarters that sends out feelers into the environment, testing every situation to see if it is threatening, enhancing, or neutral. The ego wants to expand its territory and enhance itself with power, objects, praise, and fame. It is frightened of criticism, aggression, and embarrassment and will try to protect itself. The first primitive levels of desire, aversion, and bewilderment develop into a complex web of reactions as one thing leads to another, all in a fruitless attempt to resolve our fundamental state of anxiety.

The actions of the ego create a chain reaction. Plots and subplots develop from the fundamental strategies of the ego, and the whole thing gets as complicated as a tangled mass of yarn. If you think about your life, all your relationships with family, current lovers, ex-lovers or partners, employers or employees, children, pets, and so on, and how the ego operates in these relationships, you get a sense of this demon and how it generates outer demons, demons of the mind, and demons of elation.

The ego believes it needs to control its territory and protect itself from threats, but this never resolves our fundamental anxiety. The complexity of the drama sometimes becomes overwhelming. Sometimes it is boring, sometimes it's exciting, sometimes depressing, and sometimes scary; it's a roller coaster of emotions unfolding due to our primal angst and the strategies of the ego.

The belief that the ego must protect itself can be undermined by feeding, not fighting, the demons. Machig and Milarepa didn't play the ego's game by defending their territory when the nagas attacked; by offering their bodies, they resolved the dualistic split and liberated themselves from the ego's dramas, turning the de-mons into allies. The experience of nonduality arises as the cling-ing demon of egocentricity dissolves. This is usually a long, arduous process. The ego fears its own demise and is devious in avoiding detection; our demons are the ego's worker bees.

As our spiritual path develops, the demon of ego attacks more intensely. More obstacles and trials occur when the ego is threat-ened with dissolution. On the night of the Buddha's enlighten-ment, Mara — who represents the ego in the Buddha's life — attacks him violently, trying to divert him and hook him through seduc-tion, aggression, and laziness. This is depicted in the story of the Buddha as though these were external beings. Seductive women, the daughters of Mara, represent his desire. Attacking armies try-ing to rouse his anger represent the ego's aggression, but these are demons that arose in the Buddha's mind. The Buddha was able to stay steady in his meditation and not react. He was not distracted; instead he remained stable and unperturbed. Finally Mara gave up and retreated. Then came the dawn of the Buddha's insight into the ego and attachments as the cause of suffering, which was the core of his enlightenment experience.

From this story we can see that it is *attachment* to a dualistic perception of our world, not the outer or inner experiences themselves, that generates demons. Once we break our fixation on "me" and mine," we overcome this root demon of egocentricity.

Giving form to demons and feeding them through the five-step process leads to a state of openness and awareness that offers more than just momentary relief from our psychological issues. Certainly this relative benefit can lead to healing, freedom from addictions, and so on, but its ultimate benefit is the way such awareness undermines the demon of egocentricity.

PART FOUR

DEEPENING YOUR DEMON WORK

18

DIRECT LIBERATION

Seeing the frightful transformation of Mara's army,
the Pure Being recognizes them all as a product of illusion.
There is no demon, no army, and no beings;
there is not even a self.
Like the image of the moon in water,
the cycle of the three worlds is misleading.

—*The Buddha*

IN THE PREVIOUS CHAPTER, we touched on the core demon of egocentricity and the vastness of consciousness, ideas that create the framework for understanding the key concept of this chapter: direct liberation. Once we have practiced feeding the demons for some time, we begin to become aware of demons as they form. We learn to see them coming and recognize them as they get hold of us. This makes it possible—with practice—to liberate demons as they arise without going through the five steps, by using what is called direct liberation. This most immediate and simple route to liberating demons takes you straight to the fifth step.

Direct liberation is deceptively simple. It involves becoming aware of a demon and then turning your awareness directly toward it. It is the energetic equivalent of turning a boat directly *into* the wind when sailing; the boat stops because its power source has been neutralized. Similarly, if you turn your awareness directly *into* an emotion, the emotion stops developing. This doesn't mean you are analyzing it or thinking about it, but rather turning toward it with clear awareness. At this point, if you are able to do it correctly, the demon will be instantly liberated and vanish on the spot. The technique of direct liberation is comparable to being afraid of a monster in the dark and then turning on the light. When the light goes on, we see that there is no monster. We shine the light of awareness on a demon and it disappears.

Let's take the example of a demon of jealousy. If I notice, "Ah, I'm getting jealous. My heart rate is rising. My body is tensing," and then at that moment I turn toward the energy of jealousy and bring my full awareness to it, the jealousy will pop like a balloon. When we feed a demon using the five steps, by the time you get to the fifth step, both you and the demon have dissolved into emptiness and you are resting in that space. Here we are short-circuiting the demon as it arises by meeting its energy with awareness as soon as it surfaces, going directly to the fifth step.

By training the mind we will gradually become more and more able to do this as demons arise. You might be driving to town thinking about something having to do with your children when you start to worry and get upset. At that moment you might pause and recognize, "Ah, I'm getting caught in this emotion." You can then look directly at that worried energy, turning *into* it instead of letting it carry you away. At that moment it will dissolve, leaving you to rest in the spacious awareness that naturally opens up in its place.

Another situation where you might practice direct liberation is during an interaction with other people. You might be sitting in a meeting, for instance, when you discover that an assignment you thought had been completed has not even been started. You feel irritation welling up. But when you turn your awareness into this sensation of irritation, looking right at it, it disappears, like snow melting in a mountain lake.

Because direct liberation of demons is so deceptively simple, it is particularly important not to be deceived into thinking you have liberated a demon when you haven't. If it is a strong emotion, you may have to directly liberate it several times, or you may do better to work with it using the five steps.

One way I explain direct liberation at my retreats is through an experiment. I ask people to consciously generate a strong emotion — a moment of anger, sadness, jealousy, or desire. When they get this feeling I ask them to intensify it and then turn their awareness directly into that emotion and rest in the experience that follows. You might try this to get a sense of how direct liberation works. It can be so simple and instantaneous you will distrust the result, but check back on it, and if you have done it correctly the emotion will have dissolved.

You can also practice this method on something that does not evoke a very intense emotion but still grabs the mind. You can even create your own conceptual fixation and then liberate it. To do this look at whatever is in front of you right now. Try to generate a lot of judgment and emotion about it. For example, if you are looking at a carpet you might think, "That carpet is so hideous, how could anyone have ever chosen such an ugly color?"

You could also create a positive fixation like, "I love that carpet." Or create a fear: "I really like that carpet, it's beautiful; my grandmother gave it to me, and I hope no one spills wine on it." It doesn't matter what you choose, just try to get caught up in thoughts with some attachment behind them.

Once you have generated these thoughts, notice how much of your energy is streaming out with them; check your body and notice how stressed you feel. Then turn back *into* that outgoing energy, reversing the energy flow, and look directly at the feeling generated by the thoughts. Turn the energy back to look at its source. This neutralizes it so that only awareness remains. Rest there.

When we start working with our demons, we are still so caught up in our dramas and stories we cannot see their cause. As we continue, the mud of confusion starts to settle, and we begin to be able to look directly at emotions and attachments as they arise, freeing ourselves through direct liberaton of our demons. With considerable practice the next stage becomes possible: here immediate awareness, clear and unmodified, is stable, not something you just glimpse periodically.

At this stage you don't have to "do" anything. Awareness simply meets emotions as they arise so that they are naturally liberated; you don't even have to think about it. Emptiness, clarity, and awareness are experienced as being spontaneously present. Now from the very beginning emotions don't get hold of you, they roll like water off a duck's back. This is called *instant liberation*. An emotion bubbles up but finds no foothold and dissolves. At this point we have no need for feeding demons, because awareness governs us rather than our emotions. Alas, most of us have yet to reach this level!

When we fixate on the duality of hopes and fears, we are attributing real existence to something illusory, like the monster we imagine in the dark room. We should remember that the true nature of the mind has no solidity; it is rootless, clear, radiant awareness. Knowing this, don't try to block the emotions and sensations that arise in your mind. Don't try to analyze them. Whenever thoughts or memories come up, don't hold on to them by ruminating on them. Mind itself is luminous and clear, like immeasurable space, and any feeling, thought, or memory within it is like a cloud in a clear sky. Clouds have many shapes and qualities, and so do our thoughts and emotions. But clouds do not change the sky, and if you let your mind have its transient thoughts without interference, the demons will be overcome effortlessly.

Direct liberation also occurs when you practice seeing yourself and the world as though you were living in a lucid dream — that is, dreaming and realizing you are dreaming at the same time. When you recognize the illusory, dreamlike nature of your experience of the world, demons will be liberated on the spot. This doesn't mean you should be spacey or vague, but just hold things in a lighter way, seeing them in a context of spaciousness. When you realize that most of your experience is a fabrication of the mind, there is no demon to be fed. It's already gone. The traditional analogy for this state is "a thief entering an empty house." However, most of us are not in this state; we are more like thieves entering a full house and trying to stuff everything into a bag to haul away. So although direct liberation or instant liberation is something we can work toward and aspire to, always remember that the five steps offer a method to work with the things in our bag.

Normally we empower our demons by believing they are real and strong in themselves and have the power to destroy us. As we fight against them, they get stronger. But when we acknowledge them by discovering what they really need, and nurture them, our demons release their hold, and we find that they actually do not have power over us. By nurturing the shadow elements of our being with infinite generosity, we can access the state of luminous awareness and undermine ego. By feeding the demons, we resolve conflict and duality, finding our way to unity.

You may gradually learn the practice of direct liberation, but it is important not to let go of the five-step practice of feeding your demons too soon. Working through the five steps is very important in articulating and liberating our demons. Direct liberation requires sophisticated awareness and a deep meditation practice.

19

DEMONS IN THE WIDER WORLD

Take a demon to be a demon and it'll harm you;
Know a demon's in your mind and you'll be free of it.

—*Milarepa*

RECENTLY, WHEN I was asked by one of my daughters, "What do you really want from the publication of this book?" I paused, and the image came to me of that dark, rainy summer night when I first heard the Chöd sung at Apho Rinpoche's monastery in Manali. Then I thought about what followed: learning the practice, giving up my monastic vows, marriage, children, the death of Chiara, divorce, and the gradual understanding of how Machig's teachings on feeding our demons applied to my life.

I also flashed on the world situation today, where countries and religions demonize one another. Nature itself is becoming demonic in its ever-increasing numbers of hurricanes, floods, earthquakes, droughts, and tidal waves. I thought about how we are tormented by polarization within and without, and I found myself saying, "I feel we are in desperate need of a new paradigm that inspires us to stop fighting against ourselves and each other. I would like to see a world in which people no longer think that the best alternative is to destroy whatever opposes them. I think

Machig's teachings have something profound to offer, and I want to make her teachings accessible both on the personal and the collective level."

I hope this book contributes in some small way to recognizing how we create our enemies, which may give us the ability to resist demonizing others. If we persist in thinking of other people, groups, countries, or races as evil, we will be caught in an unending battle with them. But if we can make the revolutionary shift from fighting to feeding the very forces that seem most threatening, we will make a major impact on our world.

Throughout this book I have focused mainly on personal demons, with the idea that the influence we cast on the world begins with ourselves. We've seen that what we perceive as an outer demon is often something in ourselves. We've also learned to focus on our reaction to outer events, rather than seeing the situation or person as the demon. Understanding our inner demons can help us to manage the torrent of thoughts and emotions that flows through our minds regardless of outer events.

At this point we are ready to extend the analogy of feeding the demons beyond ourselves, to consider demons in families, communities, the workplace, organizations, and nations. In this chapter we'll look at how demons work in the world as it extends out from ourselves, like ripples from a rock thrown into a pond.

The process of acknowledging our collective demons begins with our personal demons—fears, paranoia, prejudices, arrogance, and other weaknesses. Families, groups, nations, and even society as a whole can create demons that are the sum of our unresolved individual demons. If we do not acknowledge our personal demons, our weaknesses and fears can join those of others to become something monstrous.

Groups can also project their demons onto individuals or minorities within their group. If someone in a group acts out, the group can place blame on that person, even if that individual may be expressing something unspoken that is present in the group. When a group tries to portray itself as all good, it needs to find someone onto whom to project its shadow.

Since ancient times the scapegoat has served as a way of projecting group demons onto an individual. Someone was chosen to carry the unlived, dark, and repressed side of the group, and in earlier times this scapegoat would have been ritually sacrificed by the group. Later the scapegoat took on a more symbolic form and was destroyed in effigy. We still see remnants of this ritual in Carnival celebrations and in modern versions. The Burning Man festival in Nevada is one such example, where as many as twenty-five thousand people gather yearly to express themselves artistically, and at the end of the gathering an effigy is burned. These are symbolic, collective ways to work with the scapegoat.

Sometimes collective demons are incorporated into cultural rituals, which make the group aware of the collective demon by bringing it "out of the closet." In many native cultures, jesters act contrary to the social norms, breaking cultural taboos, expressing the forbidden. In Bhutan, at the religious festivals called *tsechu*, a clown with a huge penis makes fun of people, giving expression to the repressed sexual aspect of the culture. During Carnival and at some North American tribal gatherings, clown figures also do shocking, forbidden things. In this way collective demons are released in a culturally accepted form, taking pressure off the group.

When we unknowingly project our demons onto a group or individual scapegoat, this can have tragic consequences. To avoid the consequences of such scapegoating, we must become attuned to the moment when a scapegoat is being created. For example, if a family has one member who is upsetting the family and everyone else starts to agree that that person is the problem, a family scapegoat has been created.

Throughout history human beings have had the tendency to demonize other groups who are in some way different from themselves. Demonizing large groups is essential to the war machine, for example. If we think of the enemy as demonic rather than as individuals with mothers.ers, spouses, and children, we can more easily kill without hesitation or remorse.

When a collective demon is able to possess us, it means that we have in ourselves some aspect of whatever we are reacting to. Heterosexuals who attack homosexuals have a fear of homosexual tendencies in themselves. Without this fear they wouldn't have such an emotionally charged reaction. The antidote is awareness; when personal demons are unconscious, collective demons have a greater possibility of gaining control.

COLLECTIVE DEMONS IN THE FAMILY

In a family the scapegoat might be a teenager who is acting out and rejecting the family's values. This teenager may be sent away or suppressed, but until family members realize they must face their own demons, the family matrix cannot heal.

Bill, Karen, and their children, Jesse and Ariana, "had it all" materially, but there was trouble in paradise. Jesse had been problematic since childhood. He had been sent to psychiatrists, put on medication, and sent to a special school. By the time he became a teenager, Jesse was still unmanageable. He was sent away to a military boarding school, but he ran away, and by the time he was eighteen he was getting into more and more trouble. His sister, Ariana, was living with her boyfriend and working in a nearby town, and she wanted nothing to do with her family, so Jesse had few places to turn for help.

Karen was desperate to find a solution, for she felt her family was being destroyed by Jesse. When Bill and Karen went into therapy with a couples therapist trained in feeding your demons, the therapist worked with them to expose their root demons. It emerged in therapy that for Karen, Jesse was the son she had longed for, and she adored him. For Bill he was a threat to his bond with Karen; Bill was jealous of the way Karen doted on Jesse and felt she neglected him. Ariana felt she'd lost her mother to her brother, so she hated Jesse. Karen was caught in the middle and confused about the situation, and she allowed her husband and daughter to express their negativity toward Jesse.

Jesse reacted by being difficult, so he became a scapegoat for all the unresolved emotional dynamics in the family. Jesse was "the problem," which allowed everyone else to be just fine. The more difficult he became, the more justified the anger of Ariana and Bill seemed. It was truly a vicious circle.

The stigma of being a "bad apple" was withdrawn from Jesse when his parents began their demon-feeding practice. Karen worked with her demon of guilt, and Bill worked with his demons of anger and fear of abandonment. Through this practice they began to see they had turned Jesse into a scapegoat, and they addressed their own issues and their dynamics as a couple with their therapist. Jesse's behavior settled down when he was no longer carrying the family demons all by himself, and gradually the family began to communicate better and came back together.

As a scapegoat, Jesse was carrying the demons of the whole family. In order to correct this, family members had to begin to work with the demons the teenager brought up in them, as well as try to understand Jesse. This allowed a shift to occur. The same holds true in any family where a "demon" has been identified.

ORGANIZATIONAL DEMONS

Businesses and organizations often develop particular demons when they are founded and fifteen years down the line still have the same problem. For example, a company with a fear demon creates a closed system in which people are afraid to make decisions. Employees are afraid of giving feedback to managers, and of being written up for minor infractions. Thinking together about the organization's demons can be a helpful way for employees and management to clear the air.

Often the demons of the CEO or founder of an organization are infused into the organization and its employees. It is very difficult to root out these demons, which is why it is so important for owners, managers, and directors to do their own demon work as well as participate in group processes.

Sherry worked for a spa that offered clients high-quality therapies to relieve their stress. Ironically the spa was a very stressful place to work, because the owners were constantly in crisis mode. During a staff meeting, Sherry suggested looking at the company's demons, and the owners agreed to bring in a consultant trained in working with organizational demons for a daylong staff retreat. The owners were aware that stress had been present in the company from its inception and were motivated to make a change. At the retreat each employee and the owners worked separately with their own outer demons related to the company, led by a facilitator who took them through the five steps of feeding the demons. When they got back together as a group, they compared demons and allies.

There was a lot of laughter, and everyone was able to use their demons to talk about difficult things. The group heard from everyone about what their demons needed and what their allies had suggested. Then the whole group wrote suggestions for improving their organization on a large flip chart. At the end of the retreat, the facilitator used these notes to help the owners create a plan of action for feeding the company's organizational demons.

Three months later the company gathered to discuss if and how its demons had shifted, and whether or not the suggestions of the allies were being followed. For the first time in the fifteen-year history of the company, the owners were able to say they were not feeling stressed, and the employees also felt a significant difference.

Looking at collective demons in the organizations we are

connected to and being aware of scapegoats can both be ways to gain insight into the fundamental dynamics that are creating conflict in these groups.

POLITICAL DEMONS

Looking at the issue of collective demons on a larger scale, we see the power of the Western hero myth is very much evident in politics today. In the world situation, the practice of declaring war on terrorists and killing them has proven ineffectual. When we kill one terrorist, we create ten more. Today Americans are in much greater danger of terrorist attacks than we were before the start of a war in Iraq that was supposed to make us safer. We are like Hercules, who cut off one of the Hydra's heads only to find many more springing up in its place.

Only when we find a path that is effective in dealing with conflict will we accomplish what we as a nation say we want: to help others to become free, and to make the world a safer place. We know we want peace personally and collectively, but we don't know how to get there. Machig Labdrön's teachings provide us with a way to make a fundamental shift in strategy.

A collective demon can become a raging force in which individual people function like cells in the demon's body. The monster takes on a life of its own, and individuals are carried along with it. These individuals may not even realize how they have helped to create the monster. As both history and contemporary life so tragically underscore, collective demons can lead to genocide and other horrors that ordinarily would be unimaginable. If each person took responsibility for his or her demons, the sources

of mass demons and abominations like the Holocaust, and geno-
cides in Rwanda, Serbia, and Darfur, would be eliminated at their
roots. When demons are fed in political situations, the social effects can be far-reaching.

An interesting example can be seen in the story of Amilcar
Cabral, an African leader in the independence movement of
Guinea-Bissau in the 1970s. His captured Portuguese prisoners
were not tortured; instead he fed them well, treated them hu-
manely, and talked to them extensively about the need for
Guinea's independence from Portugal. He did not demonize the
opposition, but reached out to the Portuguese settlers and, via
radio, to the Portuguese at home. He did this in much the same
way Gandhi responded when the British officer came to threaten
him with arrest.

Once released, Cabral's Portuguese prisoners became allies of
Cabral's cause and helped with the revolution. Although the revolution was not peaceful, Cabral's tactics inspired a humane approach toward prisoners during the conflict, something we could
perhaps learn from today. And in fact some of the Portuguese soldiers who received this treatment from Cabral later returned to
Portugal and used the same approach in Portugal's peaceful revolution, called the Carnation Revolution, in 1974.

After the end of apartheid in South Africa, the Truth and
Reconciliation Council also used elements of the practice of feeding the demons. Perpetrators on both sides were encouraged to
apply for amnesty to a council of legal professionals who questioned them about their crimes. The crucial requirement was that
these amnesty seekers would have to share every detail of their

criminal acts, and their testimonies would be shown on television. If it was judged that they had made a full confession and were truly remorseful, they could be granted amnesty.

Afterward some of these perpetrators, at their request, met with their victims or their families, to make amends and acknowledge the suffering they had perpetrated. This approach was a revolutionary way to avoid the usual bloodbath that follows political change after generations of violent oppression. Instead of demonizing the perpetrators and continuing the cycle of violence, the Truth and Reconciliation Council offered compassionate witnessing, a revolutionary alternative to revenge.

As we consider the challenge of understanding collective demons and how they work, it is important for us to remember that the only way to stop collective demons is by becoming aware of our own demons. By doing our own work we are less likely to get swept up by a collective demon in the first place. The personal becomes global.

Most cultural and spiritual traditions manage demonic forces or enemies by acknowledging the need for protection. In these pages I have suggested that by directing your attention inward toward the real culprit—egocentricity—there is less need to protect yourself from evil. Instead of praying to be protected, offer compassion, and even the most ferocious demons can become your greatest allies. This is the fundamental turnaround that could lead to global peace.

Do not be fooled by the idea that demons are external to us. We are seeing our own mind projected in living color all around us. Train yourself to see things this way. Generate love and compassion toward whatever demon appears—without or within. When you finally understand from your own experience that there is no need to cater to the concerns of the ego, you will no longer cling to hopes and fears, or gods and demons. You will see that the source of your pain is clinging to your ego. You will rest in the limitless expanse of awareness—your true home. And you will be free.

Through shifting our worldview from one of attacking our enemies and defending our territory as Hercules did, to one of feeding our demons, we can learn to stay in dialogue with the enemy and find peaceful solutions. This was the path of Machig, Gandhi, and Cabral. In this way we begin a quiet revolution. Drawing on the inspiration of the teachings of an eleventh-century yogini, we can change our world. Preserving and developing Machig Labdrön's teachings in the West is a great privilege and joy. I pray some of her wisdom seeps out through these pages and inspires you to transform your demons into allies through the ultimate act of generosity.

May all beings benefit.

FROM MACHIG'S LAST INSTRUCTIONS

. . . Mind itself, [natural and co-emergent]
Has no support, has no object:
Let it rest in its natural expanse without any fabrication.
When the bonds [of negative thoughts] are released,
You will be free, there is no doubt.

As when gazing into space,
All other visual objects disappear,
So it is for mind itself.
When mind is looking at mind,
All discursive thoughts cease
And enlightenment is attained.

As in the sky all clouds
Disappear into sky itself:
Wherever they go, they go nowhere,
Wherever they are, they are nowhere.
This is the same for thoughts in the mind:
When mind looks at mind,
The waves of conceptual thought disappear.

As empty space
Is devoid of form, color or image,
So too, mind itself
Is free of form, color or image.

As the heart of the sun
Cannot be veiled by an eternity of darkness
So too, the realization of the ultimate nature of the mind
Cannot be veiled by an eternity of sāmsara.

Even though empty space
May be named or conventionally defined,
It is impossible to point it out as "this."
It is the same for the clarity of mind itself:
Although its characteristics may be expressed,
It cannot be pointed out as "this."

The defining characteristic of mind
Is to be primordially empty like space;
The realization of the nature of the mind
Includes all phenomena without exception.

.   .   .   .

Abandoning all bodily activities,
Remain like a bunch of straw cut loose.
Abandoning all verbal expressions of speech,
remain like a lute with its strings cut through.
Abandoning all mental activity,
That is Mahāmudrā.

In the Dharma tradition of this old lady
There is nothing to do other than this.

Ah, fortunate heirs and disciples gathered here,
This body of ours is impermanent like a feather on a high mountain
  path,
This mind of ours is empty and clear like the depth of space.
Relax in that natural state, free of fabrication.
When mind is without any support, that is Mahāmudrā.
Becoming familiar with this, blend your mind with it—
That is Buddhahood.

. . . .

Right now you have the opportunity.
Look for the essence of mind—this is meaningful.
When you look at mind, there's nothing to be seen.
In this very not seeing, you see the definitive meaning.

. . . .

This old lady has no instructions more profound than this to give you.

—From *Jérôme Edou*, Machig Labdrön and the Foundations of Chöd

ABBREVIATED VERSION OF THE FIVE STEPS OF FEEDING YOUR DEMONS

SETTING THE STAGE

Nine Relaxation Breaths

Close your eyes and keep them closed until the end of the fifth step. Take nine deep relaxation breaths with long exhalations. For the first three breaths, breathe in and imagine the breath is traveling to any tension in the body, then release this tension with the exhalation. For the second three breaths, inhale into any emotional tension, feel where you hold it in your body, and release it with the exhalation. And last, breathe into any mental tension, feeling where you hold nervousness, worries, or mental blockages in your body and releasing them with the exhalation.

Motivation

Generate a heartfelt motivation to practice for the benefit of yourself and all beings.

STEP 1: FIND THE DEMON

- Decide which demon, god, or god-demon you are going to work with.
- Locate where you hold it most strongly in your body and intensify the sensation.
- Become aware of the qualities of the sensations in your body including: color, texture, and temperature.

STEP 2: PERSONIFY THE DEMON AND ASK IT WHAT IT NEEDS

- Personify this sensation as a figure with arms, legs, and eyes and see it facing you. If an inanimate object appears, imagine what it would look like if it were personified as some kind of animate being. Notice color, skin surface, gender, size, its character, its emotional state, the look in its eyes, and something about the demon you didn't see before.

- Ask the demon:

  What do you want from me?
  What do you need from me?
  How will you feel if you get what you need?

- Having asked the questions, immediately change places with the demon.

APPENDIX

STEP 3: BECOME THE DEMON

- Face the chair or cushion you were seated on and become the demon, allowing yourself a little time to "sit in its shoes."
- Notice how your normal self looks from the demon's point of view.
- Now answer the three questions:

What I want from you is . . .
What I need from you is . . .
When my need is met, I will feel . . .

STEP 4: FEED THE DEMON AND MEET THE ALLY

Feeding the Demon

- Come back to your original position. Take a moment to settle in and see the demon in front of you.
- Dissolve your body into nectar that has the quality of the *feeling* that the demon would have if its need was satisfied (this is the answer to the third question in step three).
- Feed the demon to its complete satisfaction, imagining the nectar entering the demon any way you wish. Keep feeding until complete satisfaction is reached (if the demon seems to be insatiable, then imagine how it would look if it were completely satisfied). At this point you can go directly to step five or meet your ally.

Meeting the Ally

- If there is a being present in place of the demon when you end the fourth step, ask this being if it is the ally. If it is not, invite an ally to appear. If the demon has dissolved completely, then simply invite an ally to appear.

- Notice all the details of the ally: its color, its size, and the look in its eyes.
- Ask it one or all of these questions:

How will you help me?
How will you protect me?
What pledge or commitment do you make to me?
How can I gain access to you?

- Change places, become the ally, and answer the question(s) above, speaking as the ally.

I will help you by . . .
I will protect you by . . .
I pledge I will . . .
You can gain access to me by . . .

- Return to your original position, then take a moment and feel the help and protection coming from the ally to you, and then imagine the ally is dissolving into you. You and the ally dissolve into emptiness, which naturally takes you to the fifth step.

STEP 5: REST IN AWARENESS

- Rest in the state that is present when the ally dissolves into you and you dissolve into emptiness. Let your mind relax without creating any particular experience. Rest as long as you like without filling the space, not trying to make anything happen or rushing to finish.

FURTHER READING

THOSE WHO wish to look further into the life and teachings of Machig Labdrön can find material of interest in my book *Women of Wisdom* (Routledge and Kegan Paul, 1984; reissued in 2000 by Snow Lion Publications), which includes Machig's biography and was the first translation of her life story. It contains a lengthy personal preface, an introduction about women in Buddhism, some introductory material on Chöd and the four demons, and the biographies of five additional women teachers from Tibet.

Machig Labdrön and the Foundations of Chöd, by Jérôme Edou (Snow Lion, 1995), presents another translation of Machig's biography, as well as substantial related material on Chöd and its origins.

Machik's Complete Explanation: Clarifying the Meaning of Chöd, a translation of a Tibetan text with this name, along with an excellent scholarly introduction and commentaries by the translator and editor, Sarah Harding, was published in 2003 (Snow Lion). This book includes the life of Machig, more of her teachings, and specific question-and-answer discussions with her principal students.

The first Western reports of Chöd came from a French adventurer who lived in Tibet, Alexandra David-Neel, in her book about travels in Tibet titled *Magic and Mystery in Tibet* (1932; reprinted in 1971 by Dover Publications). This account provides a rather dramatic impression of the practice.

W. Y. Evans-Wentz published the first translation of a Chöd liturgy in his 1935 book *Tibetan Yoga and Secret Doctrines* (Oxford University Press, 1967). The book provides an interesting sense of how the West saw Tibetan Buddhism in the first part of the twentieth century. Evans-Wentz was responsible for some of the first significant translations of Tibetan texts.

Anila Rinchen Palmo translated several essays about Chöd in *Cutting Through Ego-Clinging* (Montignac, France: Dzambala, 1987).

Giacomella Orofino's piece called "The Great Wisdom Mother" was included in *Tantra in Practice* (Princeton University Press, 2000), edited by David Gordon White. In addition, she published articles on Machig Labdrön in Italian.

RESOURCES

FOR MORE INFORMATION on feeding your demons as well as retreats teaching this approach, please visit www.kapalatrain ing.com or e-mail info@kapalatraining.com. The Web site offers a variety of resources related to Kapala Training, feeding your demons, and the teachings of Tsultrim Allione and Machig Lab-drön. The site also includes supplementary articles, free materials, listings of local practice groups, a schedule of upcoming events, answers to FAQs, and other features. You'll find information on Tsultrim Allione's national and international events and retreats, which offer continuing education units to teachers, social work-ers, and health-care professionals. Tara Mandala's bookstore of-fers audio and DVD programs on feeding your demons. See our Web site or call 970-731-3713, ext. 1.

In 1993 Tsultrim Allione founded Tara Mandala, a 700-acre retreat center in southwest Colorado, to further the transmission of Buddhist practices in the Western world. The center provides short- and long-term Buddhist retreats as well as other programs from various traditions and disciplines. For schedules and other information, please contact us at:

Tara Mandala
P.O. Box 3040
Pagosa Springs, CO 81147
Phone: 970-731-3711
Fax: 970-731-4441
E-mail: info@taramandala.org
Web site: www.taramandala.org

ACKNOWLEDGMENTS

FIRST AND foremost, my gratitude goes to Machig Labdrön, whose teachings form the basis of the ideas expressed in this book, and whose life story is woven throughout it. In a world where models of enlightened women are rare, Machig stands as an example of a fully realized woman, and her impact is still being felt nearly a thousand years after her life. Machig is the only woman credited with founding her own spiritual lineage in Tibet, a lineage that has passed from teacher to student down through the generations to this day.

As I set myself to the task of presenting teachings of Tibetan Buddhism authentically yet in a way that benefits the contemporary mind in the context of a modern global reality, I have been continually inspired by His Holiness the Fourteenth Dalai Lama. He is a true gift to all of humanity; may his lotus feet remain upon the earth always. Deep bows of gratitude also to my root teachers of Chöd, Apho Rinpoche and Gegyen Khyentse, as well as heartfelt thanks to Rinpoche's wife, and my dear friend, Amala Urgyen Chödrön, for being an example of a mother who was also a serious Buddhist practitioner and for giving me my first Chöd drum.

I thank Chögyal Namkhai Norbu Rinpoche for teaching me the real meaning of Chöd and the four demons, and for his vision in transmitting the profound Dzog Chen teachings in the West. He helped me understand the Chöd as a practice I could apply directly to the issues in my life. Thanks also to Lodrö Rinpoche in Zurich for conversations about the application of the four demons in Western life and further Chöd empowerments.

Adzom Rinpoche gave me incredible teachings on Chöd, opened the gate to Troma, the Fierce Mother, and brought me an understanding of *dulzhug*, the way of confronting demons that pushes us to greater depths. He has been a luminous presence in my life and a blessing for Tara Mandala. Gratitude also to Karma Dorje Rinpoche from Zangri Kangmar in Tibet for his profound gifts, and to Lama Wangdu Rinpoche, the embodiment of generosity and joy, and holder of Machig's lineage.

My agent, Anne Edelstein, had instant confidence in the book and has had a steadfast commitment to my work. Tracy Behar, my editor at Little, Brown and Company, immediately understood the importance of the ideas expressed here. Thanks to Jennifer Lauck, who introduced me to them both. Peter Guzzardi contributed his editing skills and his belief in the revolutionary paradigm shift proposed in the book. Gratitude to Peggy Leith Anderson, for incredibly skillful copyediting and for her heartfelt connection to the book. Kimberley Snow spent several weeks one winter working with me on the book proposal, and cooking gourmet meals at the same time. Thanks to those who transcribed, edited, read, or otherwise helped with the various stages of this book. To name a few: Julia Jean, Brian Hodel, Karen Meador, Claudia Webinger, Barbara Staemmler, Leslie Barnett, Diane Hyde, Peter Weinstein, Mary O'Beirne, Belinda Griswold, Rachel Nave, Ravenna Michalsen, and Yamuna Becker. My son-in-law, director-screenwriter Trevor Sands, did a close reading of the manuscript and offered his comments at a critical moment. Thanks to the Camino Militar crew — Andrew Ungerleider, Gay Dillingham, and Donna Boner — for sweet sunsets, refuge, love, and rest in Santa Fe. Thanks to Jim Gollin and Van Jones for the story of Amilcar Cabral.

I also want to acknowledge Professor Anne Klein, PhD, and Harvey Aronson, PhD, for conversations at key times about the interface of Eastern and Western wisdom. Many thanks to all of my friends who contributed their demon stories (I have changed names and details to protect their privacy); without your help and generosity, the living examples of people's experience with the practice would not be in these pages. My thanks to resident staff of Tara Mandala for contributing their demon stories and for supporting me in all ways and through their love, skill, and efficiency giving me the freedom to write.

My children, Sherab, Aloka, and Cos, offered the perspective of their generation and insisted that this book was needed in our world. Deepest of all, heartfelt thanks to my husband, David Petit, for his infinite love, wise advice, and steady support throughout the writing of this book.

INDEX

egocentricity, demon of
  anxiety and, 228–31
  dualism and, 228, 229–30, 232,
    233–34
  ego-clinging and, 225–27, 233,
    253
  generating motivation and, 54
  Machig on, 108, 113
  projections and, 227
  as root of suffering, 22, 226,
    233
  as source of other demons, 109–10,
    113, 226, 232, 252
  as strategizer, 229
  vastness of consciousness and,
    230–32, 237
ego inflation, 109, 112, 113, 219–20,
  224
elation, demons of
  abuse of power and, 211, 222
  dreams and, 223
  drugs and, 223
  Machig on, 108, 112, 217, 219
  spiritual success and, 109, 112,
    217, 219–24
  worldly prestige and, 109, 217,
    218–19, 224
emotional tension, 54
emotions
  abuse demons and, 173
  addiction demons and, 165
  direct liberation of, 238–41
  egocentricity demon and, 233
  family demons and, 183
  finding demon and, 56, 58
  in five-step process, 81–82
  hydras and, 91
  illness demons and, 126–27
  inner demons and, 111
  mind demons and, 194
  release of, 6
  social phobia and, 137
  witness and, 84
emptiness, dissolving into, 6
enemies
  creation of, 244
  destroying, 19–20, 243–44, 253

  engaging with, 17, 20
  inner enemies, 3
energy, freeing up, 116–17, 230
epidemics, 118, 119, 221

family demons
  collective demons and, 246–48
  depression demons and, 180,
    205–6
  hydras and, 188, 190
  illness and, 183–85
  mother-lineage and father-lineage
    demons, 180–81, 188, 190–92,
    198
  multigenerational demons,
    185–88
  as outer demons, 109
  perpetuation of, 188–90
  relationship demons and, 160
  sexual abuse and, 180, 181–83
  social phobia and, 190
father-lineage demons, 180–81, 188,
  190–92, 198
fear. *See also* phobias
  acceptance of, 150
  of aging, 116, 140–41
  of death, 139–41
  illness demons and, 121–24, 125,
    134
fear, demon of
  abuse demons and, 174–75, 178,
    179
  avoiding certain situations and,
    135–36
  death/loss and, 139–41
  as family demon, 180, 190–91
  finding demon and, 56
  five-step practice and, 138, 148,
    149, 150
  hopes based on, 6, 114–15
  illness and, 121–24
  organizational demons and, 248
  as outer demon, 109, 136
  panic demon and, 148–50
  post-traumatic stress disorder and,
    142–48
  social phobia demons, 136–39

ABOUT THE AUTHOR

TSULTRIM ALLIONE, MA, was raised in New England and has been studying Tibetan Buddhism since 1967. She was one of the first Americans to be ordained as a Tibetan nun. She was ordained in 1970 by the Sixteenth Karmapa, Rangjung Rigpe Dorje, who recognized her in a crowd when she was twenty-two. After ordaining her in Bodhgaya, India, he predicted she would benefit many beings.

After four years as a nun, she returned her monastic vows, married, and had three children, while earning a master's degree in Buddhist Studies/Women's Studies from Antioch University. At this time she wrote *Women of Wisdom*, a groundbreaking book on the lives of great women Tibetan practitioners. She has continued throughout her life to practice, study, and teach, traveling worldwide to teach and lead pilgrimages as well as spending long periods in personal retreat whenever possible.

Inspired by a vision she had in her youth, while living in the Himalayas, of a Western retreat center where the depths of meditation experienced in Tibet would be possible, in 1993, with her husband, David Petit, Tsultrim founded Tara Mandala, a 700-acre retreat center where she is now the spiritual director and resident teacher. A three-story mandala-shaped temple, residence building, community building, and numerous retreat cabins and small residences have been constructed on this special land to create opportunities for long- and short-term retreat. The library there is a repository of wisdom literature. The land itself has been designated as a *ney*, or power place, by many visiting Tibetan lamas, and as *tersa* land, where *termas* (secret treasures) are revealed. Retreats such as Kapala Training, Chöd, and Green Tara, as well as other teachings and retreats, take place at Tara Mandala.

The lineages held at Tara Mandala are those of Machig Labdrön, Nyingtig, and Ösel Dorje Sang Dzö, the secret treasure cycle of Adzom Drukpa, Pawo Dorje, through her teacher Adzom Rinpoche. One of her main focuses now is to find and restore the teachings of Machig Labdrön.